CUCINA di
AMALFI

CUCINA di AMALFI

SUN-DRENCHED RECIPES FROM ITALY'S MOST MAGICAL COASTLINE

Ursula Ferrigno

with photography by
NASSIMA ROTHACKER

Illustrations by Colin Elgie

RYLAND PETERS & SMALL
LONDON • NEW YORK

Dedication

To Nicola, my sister, for being so invested in this project for me and for helping with writing recipes, with historiography and for supporting me through this fabulous journey.

Senior Designer Toni Kay
Senior Editor Abi Waters
Head of Production Patricia Harrington
Creative Director Leslie Harrington
Editorial Director Julia Charles

Illustrator Colin Elgie
Food Stylists Eleanor Mulligan
  and Troy Willis
Prop Stylist Lauren Miller
Indexer Vanessa Bird

First published in 2023 by
Ryland Peters & Small
20-21 Jockey's Fields, London
WC1R 4BW
and
341 E 11th St
New York, NY 10029

10 9 8 7 6 5 4 3 2 1

Text © Ursula Ferrigno 2023
Design and commissioned photography
© Ryland Peters & Small 2023
(see page 191 for full details)

Printed in China.

ISBN: 978-1-78879-508-1

A CIP record for this book is available from the British Library.
US Library of Congress cataloging-in-Publication Data has been applied for.

NOTES

- All spoon measurements are level unless otherwise specified.
- All eggs are medium (UK) or large (US), unless specified as large, in which case US extra-large should be used. Uncooked or partially cooked eggs should not be served to the very old, frail, young children, pregnant women or those with compromised immune systems.
- When a recipe calls for cling film/plastic wrap, you can substitute for beeswax wraps, silicone stretch lids or compostable baking paper for greater sustainability.
- When a recipe calls for the grated zest of citrus fruit, buy unwaxed fruit and wash well before using.
- Ovens should be preheated to the specified temperatures. If using a fan-assisted oven, adjust temperatures according to the manufacturer's instructions.
- To sterilize preserving jars, wash them in hot, soapy water and rinse in boiling water. Place in a large saucepan and cover with hot water. With the saucepan lid on, bring the water to the boil and continue boiling for 15 minutes. Turn off the heat and leave the jars in the hot water until just before they are to be filled. Invert the jars onto a clean dish towel to dry. Sterilize the lids for 5 minutes, by boiling or according to the manufacturer's instructions. Jars should be filled and sealed while they are still hot.

MIX
Paper from
responsible sources
FSC® C106563

CONTENTS

INTRODUCTION

La Costiera Amalfitana, the Amalfi Coast, is also known as *la divina costiera*, 'the divine coast'. And to me this is no surprise, because the whole area is magical, with its vertiginous terraces, historic churches and villas, pastel-painted villages clinging to the cliffs, all suspended between a clear blue sky and the sapphire waters of the Mediterranean. The Amalfi Coast is also where I was born and where I lived until I was 12 years old. Our home is the village of Minori, one of the 13 villages officially included in the *costiera*. Even after we moved to the UK, we would return to Italy every summer to be with my grandparents. To me it was, and still is, a paradise – if a little busier now than it was during my childhood!

CAMPANIA & THE AMALFI COAST

The Amalfi Coast is in Campania, one of the southernmost regions of Italy. It is known as *Campania Felix* – 'happy countryside' – and I think most of us are indeed happy, living in such a beautiful place, not far from Naples, the lively capital. The villages that dot the Amalfi Coast are, from the west: Positano, Praiano, Furore, Conca dei Marini, Amalfi, Atrani, Ravello, Minori, Maiori, Cetara and Vietri sul Mare; Tramonti and Scala are inland, in the mountains. Often the nearby Salerno, Sorrento, Capri and Naples are associated with the Amalfi Coast, and certainly in a culinary sense they are important.

The major link between most of these small municipalities is a narrow, rollercoaster of a highway, the 43 km (27 mile) *Strada Statale* 163 (SS163), which twists and turns its way along the clifftops, often single lane and with many sharp turns. The SS163 is perhaps the least amenable of the Amalfi Coast attractions. In high season the road is clogged with tourists driving from one village to another, slowing down to admire the wonderful views, resulting in horrendous traffic jams. (In 2022 the authorities instituted a traffic-calming idea that everyone hopes will help.)

The entire Amalfi Coast has been listed as an UNESCO World Heritage Site because of its unique landscape and natural beauty. Italy holds the greatest number of these heritage sites – 58 in total (to rival China's 56) – and Campania has 10 of them. The award is also based on the area's important cultural heritage. For instance, Amalfi was one of the four major maritime republics of the peninsula (along with Venice, Genoa and Pisa). The town was a major seafaring and trading hub, travelling as far afield as Constantinople

(now Istanbul), and instituted the *Tavole Amalfitane* (the 'Amalfan tables') in the 12th century, which were then a milestone in maritime law. There are many Greek and Roman sites of interest – particularly the Villa Romana in Minori. And of course the Amalfi Coast is not far from the stupendous Roman sites of Pompeii and Herculaneum to the west (both destroyed by Vesuvius in 79AD) and the Greek Paestum to the east, south of Salerno.

In Homer's *Odyssey*, the sirens sing to lure passing sailors to their doom. According to local legend, their island lies just off the Amalfi Coast. Most authorities place the sirens in the Strait of Messina, between Italy and Sicily, but a hotel in Positano is named after the sirens, so the legend must be true!

The Amalfi Coast seems to have acted as a siren song for many people, not just sailors, over the centuries. It was a popular place to visit on the Grand Tours of the 18th and 19th centuries. In the 1850s, Cosima Wagner, wife of the great German composer, described the long journey by mule to the town of Ravello, perched high above the sea. They visited the gardens of Villa Rufolo, and Richard Wagner, after 20 years of composer's block, was inspired to finish his opera *Parsifal*. Years later the town instituted a music festival in his honour, which still exists, running from June to mid-September every year.

Writers such as D.H. Lawrence, Ibsen, Steinbeck and Tolstoy visited and lauded the *costiera*. Film directors, such as Rossellini (born in Maiori), Zefferelli and Fellini used the *costiera* as a backdrop in films. While filming *L'Amore*, Rossellini shot scenes along the *sentiero dei limoni* ('pathway of the lemons'), the old trail connecting Maiori and Minori. This still exists, redolent of the past: men and women would haul lemons from the hilltop terraces down to the beaches of both villages, from which they would be shipped to the UK and America. Parts of more recent films were also shot on the Amalfi Coast, including *The Talented Mr Ripley* and *Wonderwoman*.

Crowds flock to the Amalfi Coast even now, and its villages are the playground for holidaymakers from all over the world, enjoying the peace (apart from the traffic!), the secluded beaches, the ancient stairways and narrow dark lanes, the sophisticated boutiques and the many outstanding (often very expensive) food shops and restaurants.

MINORI & LEMONS

I truly believe that I became involved in the food world because of my family, and because my family lived on the Amalfi Coast. There, 100 years ago, if you were not a fisherman you were a farmer, and growing fruit and vegetables is what my family specialized in. My *nonno*, or grandfather, Gaetano Ferrigno, was the youngest of seven children, all girls before him! He inherited the family business early and came to the UK many times selling his produce.

When my father – also Gaetano – was old enough, my *nonno* gave him £500 and told him to go off and make money for himself. Lemons were his first love: he would sail to London, armed with a multitude of crates. Family lore has it that Fleet Street and its disillusioned pressmen were granted new life by the intense flavour of Amalfi lemons in their gin and tonics! The business expanded and he started exporting Italian potatoes, broccoli, lettuces from Sicily, chickpeas, strawberries from

Paestum – he was the first person to bring radicchio to the UK. We still grow lemons – thick skinned for limoncello, the Italian liqueur, and thin skinned for juicing.

As a result of the family business and being surrounded by people who were passionate about growing and eating, during those first 12 years of my life I absorbed an enormous amount of knowledge. I grew up knowing, for instance, all about growing pears, plums, apricots, oranges and lemons. I knew how to graft lemons to get a thinner skin, or more juice, or to produce a lemon that was sweet, rather than sour, so that you could eat it like an orange! I watched my grandmother making pasta, soups, rolling meatballs, preserving tomatoes and aubergines, creating magical dishes out of a few simple ingredients, most of them specialities of the area – San Marzano tomatoes, buffalo mozzarella, anchovies, fish straight from the sea, with local olive oil. For my sisters and me, our favourite lunch was the homemade pizza on Sundays.

My grandmother cooked well, so she said, because she loved us well, and I treasure and cling to that thought. I also inherited my *nonno's* love of lemons, and still to this day, the very smell of lemons evokes the most wonderful memories, reminding me of heat and happiness, which is possibly the very essence of the Amalfi Coast and of Italy.

Ursula Ferrigno

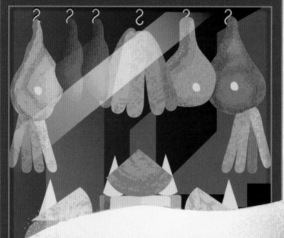

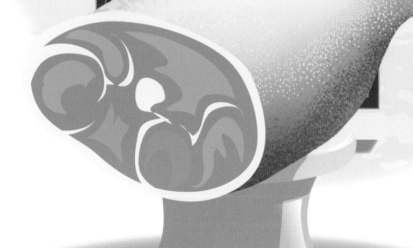

APPETIZERS

ANTIPASTI

DELIGHTFUL ANTIPASTI

It is popularly thought that the word 'antipasto' means the course that is eaten before the pasta dish. But in reality it means 'before the meal', coming from the Latin *ante pastum*. The purpose of the antipasto is to stimulate the appetite, but certainly not to satisfy it: *antipasti* must be simple, not rich or complicated, in order to allow for the appreciation of the course (or courses) to follow. Therefore tasty, light and small morsels are the order of the day.

Along the Amalfi Coast, *antipasti* are usually based on seafood – you could choose from anchovies, sardines, baby octopus, clams, mussels, squid or cuttlefish, sea urchins, tuna, prawns or whitebait. Simply visiting the local seafood market, where the fish are so fresh they almost leap out at you, will give you an idea of what the nearby restaurants will offer. The smaller fish might be deep-fried in a light batter, as with small pieces of vegetable. There might also be some *salame* or *prosciutto*, cooked vegetables, grains or pulses, *crostini*, cheese dishes and salads. *Antipasti* are perhaps more part of a restaurant menu than a fixture of a meal at home nowadays, although they often appear at family celebrations, such as weddings or christenings. I love making and serving them, with their endless possibilities and their variety of tastes, textures and colours. They don't have to just be served

as a course before your main meal of the day either – four or five together could be served by themselves as a delicious lunch, rather like the Spanish *tapas*.

I have given you three mozzarella recipes in this chapter, as mozzarella cheese is one of the food stars of Campania and the Amalfi Coast. I think the best cheeses are made here, despite rivals now appearing all over the world (from China to Scotland!). The local cheese, mainly produced near Salerno, is so respected that it bears the *Mozzarella di Bufala Campana* trademark and was given DOC status (Designation of Controlled Origin) in 1993; it also gained a Protected Geographical Status from the EU in 2008. It is made from the milk of water buffalo that roam many areas of southern Italy, principally Campania, Lazio and Puglia. Anyway, they produce milk that is low in fat, which is made into balls of cheese with a soft and

gentle flavour. The cheese takes its name from the verb *mozzare*, meaning 'to cut'; this refers to the way in which the cheesemakers 'cut' the stretchy curd by hand to make it into the familiar balls.

Buffalo mozzarella should come bathing in its own packet or tub of liquid – and should be eaten promptly, when it will ooze a little of its internal milk. It is best when newly made, so I urge you to visit the Amalfi Coast (before the summer preferably, when the tourists will be in super-abundance!) in order to truly appreciate it. To be honest, it can be a little bland, so needs a little help from other flavourings. I love it because of its coolness, which is welcome in the searing heat of the south. It is best, to my mind, in a salad from the nearby island of Capri, the *caprese*, with fabulous olive oil, sliced San Marzano tomatoes, fresh basil, salt and pepper. And another popular Amalfi Coast use of

mozzarella is *in carrozza*, translated as 'in a carriage', which are slices of mozzarella sandwiched between slices of bread and fried (see page 26). The melting stringiness of the cheese also means that it is the ideal topping for pizza, another speciality of this part of Italy.

The other culinary stars of the Amalfi Coast are anchovies, or *acciughe*, here known as *alici*. The small coastal town of Cetara is the centre of the anchovy trade and has been for centuries. The town's fishing fleet is one of the best equipped on the Amalfi Coast. The fish are caught between March and July and are served fresh in a variety of ways. In Cetara, they even have a *Notte delle Lampara* at the end of July, when the fishermen and paying guests go out in the old traditional way, in small boats, with a large lamp at the bow, which attracts the fish. Most of the *alici* catch, however, is used to make *colatura di alici*, an intensely fishy sauce, which is the modern-day equivalent of the famous Roman sauce. The fish are put in barrels, weighted down, and the 'sauce', the essence of anchovies, is squeezed out. There is a *Festa della Colatura di Alici* in early December to celebrate the new bottling. I think of *colatura* as the vanilla extract of the fish world, and although it is still a bit of an underground ingredient in the UK, I think it is on its way – it brings a dish alive, adding an extra dimension to pasta sauces, salads and grains.

PEPPER & MOZZARELLA SKEWERS

SPIEDINI DI AMALFI

This is such a simple antipasti to make, but make sure you adhere to the details. Glorious to serve at gatherings as the flavourful skewers are fun to share with guests.

2 large red (bell) peppers
50 g/3½ tablespoons
　unsalted butter
6 anchovies
1 sourdough baguette, stick or
　good-quality country-style
　bread (can be a day old)
3 tablespoons olive oil
3 mozzarella balls, drained well
2 handfuls of fresh basil
fresh flat-leaf parsley, chopped,
　to garnish
sea salt and freshly ground
　black pepper

6 metal skewers

Serves 6

Preheat the oven to 200°C fan/220°C/425°F/gas 7.

Place the red peppers on a baking sheet and roast in the preheated oven for 35–40 minutes (depending on the size of your peppers) until deflated and slightly charred. Leave to cool, then peel off the skin. Cut the flesh into 18 pieces in total.

Reduce the oven temperature to 160°C fan/180°C/350°F/gas 4.

Place the butter in a small pan with the anchovies and heat gently until the butter has melted.

Cut the bread into 18 even slices, ideally with the crusts removed and brush with the olive oil. Cut the mozzarella into 18 slices about 1 cm/½ in. thick.

Thread 6 skewers, allowing 3 pieces of each ingredient per skewer. Start with bread, then pepper, cheese and basil leaves and repeat, making sure that the ingredients are tightly pressed together. Place the skewers on an oiled baking sheet, season well and brush with the melted anchovy butter.

Bake in the preheated oven for 5 minutes, turning halfway to check that they are evenly browning. Garnish with parsley to serve.

MOZZARELLA IN A LEMON LEAF
MOZZARELLA IN FOGLIA DI LIMONE

I'm always very keen to use the leaves of the fragrant Amalfi lemon trees whenever possible. Maybe you are lucky enough to have a tree in your garden or could visit a local greengrocer to see if they have a beautiful box of Amalfi lemons that you could take a few lemon leaves from to try this dish. Lemon leaves also work well as a base when cooking fresh fish - the volatile oils in the leaves are just below the surface, and all the aromas and flavour are captured perfectly as they seep through the fish.

1 ball of fresh buffalo
    mozzarella, cut into
    bite-sized pieces
fresh lemon leaves, blanched
    to make them flexible
sea salt and freshly ground
    black pepper
lemon zest, to garnish
    (optional)
good-quality extra virgin olive
    oil and bread, to serve

Serves 4

Preheat the oven to 200°C fan/220°C/425°F/gas 7. Line a baking sheet with parchment paper.

Depending on the size of the leaves, wrap a piece of fresh buffalo mozzarella in one or more leaves, seasoning the cheese well before enclosing it within the leaf.

Place on the lined baking sheet and bake in the preheated oven for 10-12 minutes. Remove from the oven, undo the leaf to reveal the mozzarella and top with lemon zest if desired. Enjoy with fabulous oil and bread.

VARIATION: *Fig leaves can also be used filled with goats' cheese in a similar manner.*

MINI PARMESAN PANCAKES

TORTINE DI PARMIGIANO

My father grew Italian new potatoes and I grew up with him coming home and turning a handful of potatoes out of his pockets, which were quickly cooked for him to see if he approved of the flavour. This dish has many variations and can be served like a sandwich with creamy fresh spinach or cheese in the middle, or with roasted peppers or meats on the side for antipasti.

2 large old potatoes
75 g/1 cup freshly grated Parmesan cheese
1 egg
25 g/3 tablespoons plain/all-purpose flour
a little milk, for mixing
4 tablespoons olive oil
sea salt and freshly ground black pepper
fresh flat-leaf parsley, chopped, to garnish

Serves 4

Peel, then grate the potatoes into a bowl. Add the cheese, egg, flour, salt and pepper and enough milk to form a thick batter that is of a dropping consistency. Leave to stand for 15 minutes.

In a large frying pan/skillet, heat the oil, then drop in tablespoons of the mixture (you will need to cook the pancakes in batches). Fry for 7 minutes until golden brown on one side, turn and fry the second side until golden. Lower the heat and cook for a further 1–2 minutes. Drain on paper towels. Serve hot, garnished with parsley.

FRIED COURGETTE FLOWERS

FRITTELLE DI FIORI DI ZUCCA

Grow courgettes/zucchini in your garden in the summertime and marvel at their cheerful colour, making one smile as they grow. I personally like the flowers just as they are but you could fill them with a mixture of anchovies and mozzarella before sealing and frying for added flavour.

7 g/¼ oz. fresh yeast or 1 teaspoon
   dried active yeast
450 ml/1⅞ cups warm water
250 g/1¾ cups Italian '00' flour
2 tablespoons olive oil
groundnut oil, for frying
24 large courgette/zucchini flowers
sea salt and freshly ground black
   pepper
lemon quarters, to serve

Serves 4–6

Dissolve the fresh yeast in a little of the water and set aside for 10 minutes; if using dried yeast, mix with the flour. Mix the flour, water, olive oil, yeast mixture, salt and pepper well using a whisk to beat out any lumps. Cover and leave to become bubbly for about 40 minutes (the amount of time depends on the temperature around you). Stir the bubbles in the batter.

Heat the groundnut oil to a depth of 8 cm/3 in. in a deep pan to around 180°C/350°F if you have a thermometer to check. Alternatively, test to see if it hot enough by dropping in a cube of bread; if it sizzles it's ready.

Remove the stamens from the courgette flowers, dip them one at a time into the batter, shaking off the excess. Place one at a time into the hot oil, and fry until golden for 8 minutes (depending on the size of the flowers), turning once as you cook. You should be able to fit about 4 at time into the pan, so work in batches. Remove and drain on paper towels.

Sprinkle with salt and serve with the lemon to squeeze over the flowers for maximum enjoyment.

FERRIGNO ROASTED TOMATOES
POMODORI DI FERRIGNO

Tomatoes thrive in the Italian climate; the fertile soil, the water's edge and the light all being very important factors in the success of this vital crop. This method of cooking the tomatoes is a frugal but smart way of creating a dish of utter deliciousness. Selecting the right tomatoes is important; smell the stalk end for a good peppery flavour. Buy your tomatoes from a sunny climate and choose those with a good, deep, red colour.

2 garlic cloves, crushed

4 tablespoons chopped fresh
   flat-leaf parsley

30 g/4-5 tablespoons fresh
   breadcrumbs (see Note below)

2 tablespoons olive oil

a few sprigs of fresh oregano, chopped

1 tablespoon capers, finely chopped

6 large, ripe, firm tomatoes, cut in half

sea salt and freshly ground
   black pepper

2 tablespoons good-quality extra
   virgin olive oil, to serve

Serves 6

Preheat the oven to 160°C fan/180°C/350°F/gas 4.

Mix the garlic, parsley, breadcrumbs, olive oil, oregano and capers together in a bowl and season with salt and pepper.

Place the tomatoes, cut side up, in an ovenproof dish, cover them with the breadcrumb mix and bake in the preheated oven for 20-25 minutes (depending on size) until the topping is golden brown.

Anoint with the finest extra virgin olive oil and serve.

NOTE: *The amount of breadcrumbs you need for this dish will depend on the size of your tomatoes - use more or less as needed.*

MOZZARELLA 'IN A CARRIAGE'
MOZZARELLA IN CARROZZA

Although very easy to prepare, this recipe requires small touches to reach perfection.
Nonno Ferrigno would talk endlessly about the importance of doing this well. It's yet again reliant on
fabulous ingredients; the bread should be country style, with a coarse texture. This is a very purist
recipe but you may feel inclined to add skinny slices of tomato and freshly torn basil leaves.

300 g/10½ oz. mozzarella cheese, sliced
8 small slices of bread, crusts removed,
   identical in size
150 g/5½ oz. cooked ham, cut into
   4 even slices
15 g/1¾ tablespoons Italian '00'
   or plain/all-purpose flour
90 ml/⅓ cup milk
1 large/US extra-large egg, beaten
45 g/⅔ cup dried breadcrumbs
4 teaspoons olive oil
sea salt and freshly ground
   black pepper

Serves 4

Lay a slice of mozzarella cheese on four of the slices of bread and season with salt and pepper. Cover with the ham, then top with the remaining bread to make a sandwich. Place a board over the top of the sandwiches with a weight on top and leave for at least 30 minutes (or for an hour, if possible).

Place the flour, milk, beaten egg and breadcrumbs in separate shallow bowls. Dip one sandwich first in the flour, then the milk, then the egg and, lastly, in the breadcrumbs, making sure both sides are evenly coated.

Heat the oil in a frying pan/skillet until hot and fry each sandwich for about 9 minutes until golden brown, turning once. Drain on paper towels and serve immediately.

SALAD OF ROASTED PEPPERS
PEPERONI ARROSTI

This salad is eaten all over Europe. In my grandmother's kitchen it was always available
as it can be stored in jars and preserved as a salad for your store cupboard.

2 yellow (bell) peppers
2 red (bell) peppers
3 tablespoons good-quality extra virgin
   olive oil
1 tablespoon good-quality balsamic
   vinegar
1 garlic clove, crushed (optional)
sea salt and freshly ground black pepper

TO SERVE
a few sprigs of fresh oregano
fresh bread

Serves 6

Preheat the oven to 200°C fan/220°C/425°F/gas 7.

Put the peppers in a roasting tin and bake in the preheated oven for 25 minutes until blistered and slightly charred. Leave to cool.

When cool, hold the peppers over a bowl, to catch any juices, and peel off the skins. Cut the flesh into thin strips and put in a serving dish. Add the oil, vinegar, garlic, if using, salt and pepper to the bowl of pepper juice and whisk together to make a dressing.

Pour the dressing over the peppers and serve garnished with oregano. Serve with bread to mop up the juices - *fare la scarpetta* style (see page 104).

BREAD & PIZZA

PANE E PIZZA

FLOUR IN ALL ITS FINERY

Bread and pizza are two of the most important foodstuffs of Italy, and both are made from the wheat flour produced nationwide and on the vast coastal plains of Campania. Two types of flour exist, depending on the wheat: *grano duro* (hard) and *grano tenero* (soft). Breads are usually made from *grano duro* flour, because of the higher gluten content. I usually make breads and pizza bases with strong white bread flour.

Italian flours are ground to varying degrees of fineness, with the smaller the number, the finer the flour. Type 0 and 00 are the most common – 0 is used in breads and 00, the silkiest, is used to make pizzas, pastas, cakes and biscuits. But, having said all that, many breads are made with a combination of flours; it is all a matter of experimentation. Other grains and pulses are grown and ground to flour in Italy, among them buckwheat (*saraceno*), rice (*riso*), maize (*mais*), oats (*avena*), chestnut (*castagna*) and chickpea (*ceci*).

Nowhere is bread more valued than in Italy: my family used to say that a table was not laid without bread having a major place on it. There are a number of bread sayings that Italian guru, Anna del Conte, quotes: my favourite is *'é buono come il pane'* ('as warm and kind-hearted as bread'). In the old days, particularly in the south, many bread doughs were

marked with a cross before being sent to the *panetteria* to be baked (as elsewhere in the world, private homes did not possess ovens). My own *nonno* (grandfather) used to make a sign of the cross on the base of a loaf before he cut into it – it was a way of saying thank you for the food. In his house, fresh bread, the simplest white, crisp-crusted bread (which staled quickly) would accompany soups, appetizers and main plates, and would be used to mop up leftover juices and sauces – otherwise known as *fare la scarpetta* or 'mop up with a little shoe'). When a little older, bread would be used in salads and soups and crumbled to breadcrumbs, to be used as coatings, toppings and even in pasta sauces (*pangrattato*). Baguette-type bread slices would be toasted or dried for *crostini*, and rustic breads for *bruschett*a, the perfect bases for delicious toppings.

Bread has also contributed to something that is undeniably Campanian - the pizza, the ultimate bread base for a delicious topping. Originally a pizza base would have been eaten as a flatbread - its ancestor is *focaccia* - with minimal toppings. It is in the same tradition as the Umbrian *torta al testo* (bread of the tile), and the *pide* of Turkey and *pitta* of Greece. Indeed, in many restaurants on the Amalfi Coast, the bread offered will be an actual baked pizza base, with salt and olive oil on top, perhaps a bit of rosemary.

Pizza was a food of the poor, and it was the poor of Naples, the capital of Campania, who began using the new tomatoes (introduced from the Americas at the end of the 16th century) as a topping for the bread base. These in turn were topped by cheese, usually the local mozzarella. The *pizza alla napoletana* is just that, with added garlic and oregano; the *Margherita* adds basil to the mix; and *marinara* has all of these, plus anchovies (sometimes). The *margherita* is said to have been named after the Queen who bravely visited Naples in 1889 not long after a disastrous cholera outbreak. It is also claimed that the *pizza fritta* (fried pizza) - either a folded-over pizza base with a filling like a *calzone*, or a small pizza base such as I give on page 37 - was fried rather than baked because the frying process would kill off any lingering cholera bacteria more effectively.

I have fond memories of pizza from my childhood in Minori. Pizza was a Sunday treat, to be eaten outside (all other lunches during the summer were inside, with the shutters drawn). The dough would come from the bakery. My sisters and I vied to catch the eye of the handsome boy delivering the dough, and then would compete to see who could produce the finest pizza. I think I have mastered the art now, with my lemon juice addition to the dough making for a crisper crust.

The tomato that adorns Campanian pizzas is the San Marzano cultivar. It is the preserving of this that has become one of Campania's largest and most successful agriculture-based industries. All along the Amalfi coast you will see terraces of tomatoes, and every balcony or patio is festooned with green tomato vines and their gleaming scarlet fruit. These tomatoes are used fresh, in salads or sauces, or preserved by being canned, dried in the searing sun or bottled. Preserving tomatoes is a very important exercise on the Amalfi Coast.

FRIED PIZZA WITH MOZZARELLA & PEPPERS

PIZZA FRITTA DI MOZZARELLA E PEPERONI

There were many, many forms of fried doughs in Campania during the epidemic of cholera as frying food was a way of ensuring that the food was sterilized. These *fritta* are truly delicious. This elegant version (made without yeast), this is a true celebration of anchovies and mozzarella, two of the region's most wonderful ingredients, so worth shouting about.

FRITTA
200 g/1½ cups Italian '00' flour, plus extra for dusting
1 teaspoon sea salt
1 teaspoon bicarbonate of soda/baking soda
125 ml/½ cup whole milk
olive oil, for frying

ANCHOVY DRESSING
100 ml/generous ⅓ cup good-quality extra virgin olive oil, plus extra for topping
1 shallot, finely chopped
8 anchovy fillets, chopped
100 ml/generous ⅓ cup dry white wine
1 small garlic clove
handful of fresh basil leaves, torn

TOPPING
3 large red (bell) peppers
generous handful of wild rocket/arugula leaves
4 x 100-g/3½-oz. balls of buffalo mozzarella, each torn into 3 pieces
12 anchovy fillets
1 tablespoon capers in brine, rinsed in cold water
sea salt and freshly ground black pepper

Serves 6
(2 *fritta* per person)

To prepare the *fritta*, mix all the ingredients together, expect the oil for frying, in a large mixing bowl and knead well for 8 minutes. Please do not over-knead. Place the dough in a clean bowl, cover and leave the dough to relax for 1 hour.

Preheat the oven to 200°C fan/220°C/425°F/gas 7.

Prepare the red peppers for the topping. Roast the peppers in the preheated oven for about 30 minutes, depending on the size of the pepper – they should be wrinkled and blackened slightly when ready. Cool the peppers in a bowl, remove the skin when cold and cut each pepper into 6 large strips.

To prepare the dressing, gently warm all the ingredients in a small saucepan over a low heat to heat through. Transfer to a food processor or blender and mix until smooth. Season to taste.

Once rested, the dough should be ready to fry. Break off a small golf-ball sized piece of dough and roll into a thin disc on a floured surface, to about 18 cm/7 in. in diameter. Repeat with the rest of the dough until you have 16 discs (you only need 12, so enjoy the leftovers as cooking snacks!).

Heat the oil in a frying pan/skillet over a medium heat and fry the discs one at a time, shaking the pan vigorously, for about 4 minutes until the dough circle aerates and becomes crip and golden. Drain on paper towels, sprinkle with sea salt and keep warm until ready to serve.

To assemble, toss the rocket leaves in a little extra virgin olive oil. Place a piece of mozzarella on each *fritta*. Arrange the anchovy fillets and roasted pepper strips on top. Scatter over the rocket and capers and spoon the dressing over and around the *fritta*. You might like to finish with a light drizzle of extra virgin olive oil and a sprinkling of black pepper.

PROSCIUTTO & BLACK PEPPER FLATBREAD
TORTA DI PROSCIUTTO

This flatbread is a 12th-century flatbread from the region of Amalfi. I would generally describe this as a buttery prosciutto pizza. Serve hot or cold at outdoor family gatherings as a perfect sharing bread.

350 g/2½ cups strong white bread flour, plus extra for kneading

2 teaspoons sea salt

15 g/½ oz. fresh yeast or 2 teaspoons dried yeast

250 ml/1 cup water, at body temperature

2 tablespoons melted unsalted butter, plus extra for greasing

3 teaspoons freshly ground black pepper

FILLING

4 large/US extra-large eggs, hard-boiled/cooked and chopped

200 g/7 oz. Parma ham, chopped

3 tablespoons melted unsalted butter

handful of fresh flat-leaf parsley, chopped

sea salt and freshly ground black pepper

Makes 1 flatbread

Mix the flour and salt in a bowl, making a well in the centre. Dissolve the yeast in 2 tablespoons of the water and add the yeast liquid, half the butter, 2 teaspoons of the black pepper and the remaining water to the well. Mix with a wooden spoon until a solid dough ball is formed that is neither too wet or too dry.

Knead on a lightly floured surface for 10-15 minutes until the dough is smooth and elastic. Lightly butter a clean bowl, place the dough inside and cover with a damp kitchen cloth. Leave to rise for 1 hour.

Meanwhile, prepare the filling by putting the egg, Parma ham, butter and parsley in a bowl, season and set to one side.

Preheat the oven to 200°C fan/220°C/425°F/gas 7. Butter a 25-cm/10-in. round high-sided baking pan – or you can make it free form, more often than not I do.

Knock the dough back in the bowl, then turn out and knead for 2-3 minutes. Shape into a large circle. Baste with the remaining butter and fold the dough in half and reshape. Recreate the original circle and dust the surface with the remaining black pepper. Knead for 5 minutes, or until the ingredients are well incorporated. Shape the dough into a 30-cm/12-in. circle.

Place the dough in the prepared baking pan, if you are using, and press the excess dough against the sides, coming up over the top. Cover and leave to prove for 10 minutes.

Spoon the topping mixture around the edges only of the dough casing, then fold the overlapping edges of dough over the filing to enclose it and make a rolled crust. The middle will be plain dough.

Brush all over with a little extra butter and bake in the preheated oven for 25 minutes until golden brown. Remove from the oven; you might like to brush a little more butter over the top to make the dough softer. Enjoy hot, cold or warm.

GRANDMOTHER'S SPINACH BREAD
PANE DI SPINACI DELLA NONNA

The Italians eat lots of bread and are crazy about greens - this recipe combines them both. It's the sort of thing they might eat at harvest time as an all-in-one meal (the Italian equivalent of a pasty or pie), making it a good bread to take on a picnic. Feel free to change the ingredients in the middle. The spinach is traditional to Naples and its environs, but you could use cheese or cooked vegetables, or a mixture of both.

15 g/$\frac{1}{2}$ oz. fresh yeast

350 ml/1$\frac{1}{2}$ cups body temperature water

350 g/2$\frac{1}{2}$ cups strong white unbleached flour

150 g/1 cup fine semolina

2 teaspoons sea salt

350 g/12$\frac{1}{2}$ oz. fresh spinach

2 tablespoons extra virgin olive oil, plus extra for oiling

1 garlic clove, finely chopped

2 tablespoons black olives, pitted and finely chopped

1 large/US extra-large egg white, beaten with 2 teaspoons water for egg wash

handful of sesame seeds

freshly ground black pepper

Makes 1 loaf

Dissolve the yeast in a quarter of the water in a large bowl. Leave it to sit, covered, for 10 minutes until foamy.

Add the remaining water and stir well. Mix in the flour and semolina, tablespoon by tablespoon, along with the salt. Mix with your hands until a ball of dough is formed. Knead vigorously for 10 minutes, then place in a lightly oiled bowl. Leave for 1$\frac{1}{2}$ hours, covered, until doubled in size.

Meanwhile, prepare the filling. Wash and drain the spinach thoroughly, discarding any really tough stems. Put the leaves into a pan without any additional water, cover and cook over a medium heat until wilted. Drain and leave to cool. Squeeze the spinach as dry as possible, then chop really finely.

Heat the olive oil in a frying pan/skillet, add the garlic and sauté until soft. Add the chopped spinach and cook for 2-3 minutes, then add the olives and some black pepper. Remove from the heat and leave to cool completely.

When the dough has risen, punch it down in the bowl, then turn out and roll into a circle about 40 cm/16 in. in diameter. Lift the dough onto a greased baking sheet. Spoon on the spinach filling and spread it to within 2.5 cm/1 in. of the edges. Roll the dough up tightly like a Swiss roll/jelly roll, then turn the ends under to seal. Make random 1-cm/$\frac{1}{2}$-in. deep slits on the top with a knife. Brush the top of the dough with egg wash and sprinkle over the sesame seeds. Cover and leave the bread to rise for 30 minutes.

Preheat the oven to 180°C fan/200°C/400°F/gas 6.

Bake the bread in the preheated oven for 35 minutes until golden, then transfer to a wire rack. Cool well before serving. Slice on the diagonal to reveal the wonderful swirl of the filling.

AMALFI PIZZA

PIZZA DI AMALFITANA

I boldly feel that this unique recipe creates the ultimate pizza crust – the lemon juice in the dough provides an exotic crunchiness. Feel free to garnish the finished dish with courgette/zucchini flowers if liked.

50 g/heaping ⅓ cup Italian '00' flour

250 g/1½ cups fine semolina, plus extra for sprinkling

2 teaspoons sea salt

7-g/¼-oz. sachet fast-action dried yeast

1 tablespoon fresh lemon juice

1 tablespoon olive oil

200 ml/¾ cup lukewarm water

TOPPING

1 large garlic clove, thinly sliced

55 g/1 cup coarsely grated Parmesan

125 g/4½ oz. ricotta

grated zest ½ unwaxed lemon

2 tablespoons good-quality extra virgin olive oil, plus extra to serve

½–1 medium courgette/zucchini, halved lengthways and sliced into fine half-moons

generous handful of freshly torn basil leaves, plus extra to serve

110 g/4 oz. mozzarella (ideally buffalo), coarsely grated and drained on paper towels for 30 minutes

sea salt and freshly ground black pepper

Makes 2 pizzas

Combine the flour, semolina, salt and yeast in a medium bowl. Make a well in the centre and add the lemon juice and olive oil. Using a wooden spoon, mix in the lukewarm water little by little. When you have a damp, crumbly dough, squeeze the crumbs together, then turn out the dough onto a clean work surface. Knead for a good 10 minutes, after which time the dough should be smooth and soft like silk. Return the dough to a clean bowl, cover with a damp cloth and leave to rise in a warm place for at least 2 hours, or until doubled in size.

Knock back the risen dough by gently punching it to release the air trapped inside. Turn out and knead again for 4–5 minutes. Cover the dough with a clean cloth and leave to rest for 5 minutes.

Preheat the oven to 220°C fan/245°C/450°F/gas 8. Put a baking sheet in the oven to heat up.

For the topping, combine the garlic, Parmesan, ricotta, lemon zest and olive oil in a bowl, then season with salt and pepper.

Cut the rested dough in half and roll each piece out to a rough 35-cm/14-in. circle (or 32-cm/13-in. square, if that's easier).

Sprinkle the baking sheet with semolina and put one pizza base on the hot sheet. Spread the base with half the topping, scatter over half the courgette slices, then half the basil and, finally, half the grated mozzarella.

Bake in the preheated oven for 12–15 minutes until golden and bubbling. Drizzle over a glug of extra virgin olive oil and serve topped with a few extra basil leaves. Repeat with the remaining base and topping.

SAVOURY RICOTTA PIE

PIZZA RUSTICA

This savoury ricotta pie can be served as small wedges as an antipasto or in larger portions with other contorni (see pages 114–145) for a fuller meal. Ricotta is so light and digestible and absorbs other flavours so well, making this a delightful dish.

240 g/1¾ cups Italian '00' flour, plus extra for dusting
½ teaspoon sea salt
185 g/¾ cup cold unsalted butter, plus extra for greasing
90 ml/⅓ cup cold water
1 egg yolk mixed with 1 teaspoon water, to glaze

FILLING
560 g/1 lb. 4 oz. ricotta
180 g/6¼ oz. fresh mozzarella, cut into small dice
45 g/1½ oz. prosciutto, roughly chopped
55 g/2 oz. pecorino, grated
handful of fresh flat-leaf parsley, finely chopped
2 garlic cloves, crushed
3 medium eggs, lightly beaten
sea salt and freshly ground black pepper

23-cm/9-in. springform cake pan

Serves 6–8

To make the pastry, combine the flour, salt and butter in a food processor. Slowly add the water until the dough is just moistened. Turn the dough out of the bowl, wrap in cling film/plastic wrap and chill in the fridge for at least 30 minutes.

Preheat the oven to 170°C fan/190°C/375°F/gas 5. Lightly butter the cake pan.

Mix all the filling ingredients, except the eggs, together in a large bowl. Season well, then mix in the eggs.

Roll out two-thirds of the dough on a lightly floured surface, into a 3 mm/⅛ in. thick, 35-cm/14-in. round. Put the round of dough in the prepared cake pan. Spoon in the filling and smooth the top. Trim off the excess dough, leaving a 1.25-cm/½-in. border that extends above the level of the filling.

Roll out the remaining dough to 3 mm/⅛ in. thick and cut into 4-cm/1½-in. wide strips using a fluted pastry wheel or knife. Arrange the strips over the filling in a lattice pattern and trim off any excess dough. Brush the lattice strips with the egg glaze.

Bake the pie in the preheated oven for 1 hour, then cool on a wire rack. Serve warm or at room temperature.

PEPPER BISCUITS
TARALLI CON IL PEPE

These are most commonly thought of as a special dried biscuit from Puglia but are equally enjoyed in Campania where there is a festival on 7 September to celebrate their importance. Serve as a snack with drinks or with soups and salads.

190 g/scant 1½ cups Italian '00' flour
1 teaspoon sea salt
1½ teaspoons freshly ground black pepper
7 g/¼ oz. dried yeast
40 g/3 tablespoons unsalted butter, melted
2 tablespoons coarsely ground polenta/cornmeal

Makes 35-40 biscuits

Heap the flour onto a work surface and make a well in the centre. Add a pinch of salt, the pepper, yeast and butter. Stir with a fork, incorporating a little flour each time and adding water as necessary to form a ball. Knead for a good 10-15 minutes to achieve a smooth, soft dough.

Pinch off a walnut-sized piece of dough and roll into a 20-cm/8-in. length. Holding each end of the rope, twist the ends a few times in opposite directions to form a rolled cord. Seal the ends together to create a circle and place on a floured board. Continue with the rest of the dough. Cover the twists with a clean damp cloth and leave them to rise for 1½ hours. Preheat the oven to 180°C fan/200°C/400°F/gas 6.

Sprinkle 2 or 3 baking sheets with the polenta and place the twists on top. Bake for 30 minutes until golden and crisp. Leave to cool on wire racks.

TOMATO & OLIVE TARTS
POMODORO TORTE

Polenta crust pizzas - delicious, crunchy and easy, especially if you are short on time, and very impressive visually.

180 g/1⅓ cups Italian '00' flour, plus extra for dusting
80 g/heaping ½ cup polenta/cornmeal
105 g/½ cup cold unsalted butter
105 g/3½ oz. ricotta
1 large/US extra-large egg yolk

TOPPING
400-g/14-oz. can plum tomatoes
12-16 cherry tomatoes, quartered
1 tablespoon chopped fresh thyme leaves
1 tablespoon chopped fresh oregano
200 g/7 oz. goats' cheese
handful of olives, stoned/pitted
olive oil, for drizzling
basil leaves, to garnish
sea salt and freshly ground black pepper

Makes 6 individual tarts

For the pastry, put everything into a food processor and pulse briefly until the mixture comes together. Put the pastry on a floured surface and bring it together in a large lump. Divide into 6 individual pieces. Flatten a little, wrap and rest in the fridge for 30 minutes.

Meanwhile, drain the canned tomatoes in a sieve over a basin, keeping the juice for a drink, then chop the drained tomatoes.

Preheat the oven to 180°C fan/200°C/400°F/gas 6.

When the dough is chilled, roll out circles on a floured surface to 3 mm/⅛ in. thick (the dough is rustic around the edges). Top each circle with some drained tomatoes, chopped cherry tomatoes and season well. Add the thyme and oregano and crumble over some goats' cheese. Dot with olives and drizzle with a little olive oil.

Bake in the preheated oven for 20 minutes, garnish with basil and devour.

PASTA

PASTA

GLORIOUS PASTA

Pasta is synonymous with Italy, particularly Campania and the Amalfi Coast. My parents' and grandparents' houses in Minori were very close to a huge pasta factory, which I don't think exists any more. Its position was so close to the seafront that I suspect the tourism industry will have been more persuasive...

Pasta is made from wheat flour. A hard or durum wheat, also known as *semola*, is the one mostly used for pasta, both dried and fresh. In the south, though, we often use a mixture of OO plain flour and *semola*. This combination makes the pasta stronger, which is important for pasta that is to be stuffed. Most pastas are a simple amalgam of flour and water, but some are enriched with egg, and some have flavourings or colourings added (spinach for green pasta for example). Eggs are included in fresh pasta – the type you would make at home – as without them a durum-wheat pasta

would probably be too tough to roll. That said, some pastas are made with OO flours alone, mainly in the north. Dried pasta is usually made from *semola* alone, which can only be mixed and extruded by machine.

The pasta shapes most popular along the Amalfi Coast are *conchiglioni* (large shells), *scialatelli* (a short and thick ribbon), *spaghetti*, *paccheri* (hollow short tubes like *rigatoni*) and *maccheroni* (macaroni). When pasta became prevalent, the poor of Naples, who had once subsisted on cabbage, filled their bellies with macaroni, so much so that they became known nationwide as *mangiamaccheroni* (macaroni eaters)!

The sauces that accompany these pasta shapes echo the produce most available on the Amalfi Coast –

seafood and vegetables. *Spaghetti alla vongole* (clams) can be found all around the coasts of Italy, but I think its most natural home is here in Campania. The late, great Antonio Carluccio wrote of a pasta dish he ate in Positano, with *patelle e cozze* (limpets and mussels): 'It was so good, I had to have two platefuls'. *Scialatelli*, from Amalfi itself, is usually sauced with squid, mussels, prawns or clams. The pasta shape is said to have been invented in 1978 by an Amalfitano chef, but it is very likely that a version had existed in local kitchens for centuries before.

Local vegetables are used in delicious sauces: courgettes/zucchini, peas, chicory/endive, aubergines/eggplant and, of course, the famed tomatoes, whether in simple or slightly more elaborate versions, such as the *puttanesca* sauce from Naples. Its name means 'in the manner of a *puttana* (prostitute)', and is suitably hot and piquant, with its chilli, anchovy, garlic and olive content. This being the Amalfi Coast, there has to also be a pasta using Amalfi lemons in its sauce. It is a classic of the area, but with a thousand different ways of making it. I hope you enjoy mine (see page 60).

'Ndunderi is a type of gnocchi made from flour and ricotta cheese, served with a simple tomato and basil sauce. The recipe comes from Minori, my home village, and is ancient, possibly Roman. It has even been recognized by UNESCO as one of the oldest pastas. You can try it at any of the *trattorie* in Minori, but it is made every year to celebrate the feast of the patron saint of the town, Santa Trofimena, on 13 July. St Trofimena, who was Sicilian, was killed by her parents when she wanted to be baptized and become Christian. Her body was placed in a marble urn and cast into the sea. The urn miraculously did not sink, but landed on the beach at Minori. This was in the 9th century AD, and a church was built not long after, dedicated to the martyr.

Most of the pastas in this chapter are quick to prepare, using uncomplicated ingredients. Every time I make a pasta dish, I remember sitting in my grandmother's kitchen in Minori, awaiting the *pranzo* (lunch), our most important meal of the day. She would make it seem effortless, which was vital: you don't want to be slaving away in the kitchen in that searing heat. A linen-laid table, bread, water, a few *antipasti* and a steaming bowl of *pasta pomodoro*. Nothing could be more satisfactory nor, for me, more nostalgic.

MACARONI & FRESH PEAS
PASTA E PISELLI

It's well worth waiting for fresh peas to be in season for this glorious pasta dish. The mealy texture of fresh peas adds a distinct flavour that frozen peas don't have. The Italian season for fresh peas is May to June, and the English season June to August. Buy shiny, firm and bright green pods that are bulging. Peas are a great source of vitamins C and E, as well as zinc.

2 tablespoons olive oil

1 onion, finely chopped

400-g/14-oz. can plum tomatoes

2 garlic cloves, finely crushed

1 litre/quart water or vegetable broth

750 g/4¾ cups podded fresh peas

2 new potatoes, diced into 1-cm/½-in. chunks

250 g/9 oz. macaroni

generous handful of fresh flat-leaf parsley, chopped

sea salt and freshly ground black pepper

TO SERVE

generous handful of fresh basil leaves, torn

125 g/1½ cups freshly grated Parmesan (the rind can be added to the sauce for even more flavour)

good-quality extra virgin olive oil (optional)

Serves 4–6

Heat the oil in a large pan over a medium heat and sauté the onion for a few minutes until soft and golden. Add the tomatoes, garlic and water or broth, mashing the tomatoes with a wooden spoon as you stir together. Bring to the boil and simmer for a few minutes.

Add the remaining ingredients and season to your taste. Cook until the pasta and peas are al dente and the potatoes are just falling apart. This will very much depend on personal preference, so taste as you are cooking and stop when the pasta is cooked to your liking.

Serve with plenty of Parmesan cheese and freshly torn basil in warm bowls. I always like a good spoonful of extra virgin olive oil anointed on the top to serve as well.

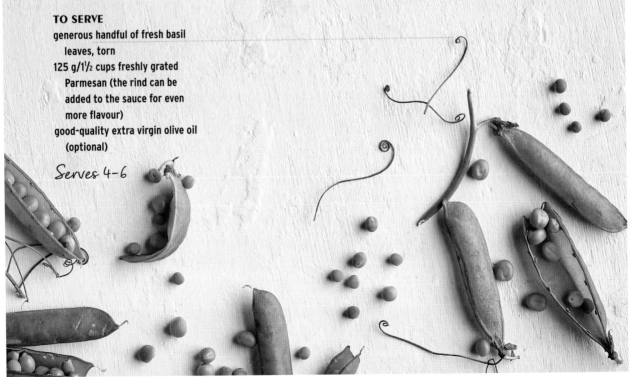

ITALIAN WHISPERS

SOFFIATINI

It is such a pleasure to make all the elements for this dish, which can be made in advance – always a help for our busy lives. This recipe is indicative of the passion for greens in Campania and is also a celebration of mozzarella.

FILLING
75 g/⅓ cup unsalted butter
75 g/generous ½ cup Italian '00' flour
200 ml/¾ cup milk
100 g/3½ oz. cooked spinach, chopped
1 teaspoon freshly grated nutmeg
generous handful of fresh flat-leaf parsley, chopped
100 g/3½ oz. buffalo mozzarella, diced
75 g/2½ oz. Parma ham, shredded
50 g/⅔ cup grated Parmesan cheese, plus extra for topping
2 egg whites, whisked until foamy
sea salt and freshly ground black pepper

PANCAKE BATTER
90 g/⅔ cup Italian '00' flour
150 ml/⅔ cup milk
2 large/US extra-large eggs, beaten
a little melted unsalted butter, for frying

Makes 6

To make the filling, melt the butter in a saucepan over a medium heat, add the flour and cook for 1 minute to make a roux. Remove from the heat and leave to cool.

In a second pan, bring the milk to the boil. Add this to the roux and cook over a medium heat until the sauce has thickened, stirring constantly. Add the spinach, nutmeg and a pinch of salt and cook for 1 more minute. Fold in the remaining ingredients and leave to cool.

To make the pancake batter, mix the flour and milk in a bowl or jug, add the eggs with a pinch of salt and mix well with a whisk.

Brush a 30-cm/12-in. heavy frying pan/skillet with melted butter and set over a medium heat. Pour a small ladleful of pancake batter into the pan and tilt the pan to make a thin pancake. Cook for about 4 minutes on each side. Repeat with the remaining batter to make 6 pancakes in total.

Preheat the oven to 180°C fan/200°C/400°F/gas 6. Brush a greased, high-sided baking sheet with melted butter.

Put a spoonful of filling in the centre of each pancake. Fold over 2 edges to meet in the centre, then fold over the other 2 edges, making a parcel. Place the pancake parcels on the prepared baking sheet, sprinkle with Parmesan cheese and cook in the preheated oven for 12 minutes until crisp and golden on top.

BUCATINI WITH COURGETTES/ZUCCHINI
BUCATINI CON ZUCCHINI

If possible, try to find Romanesco courgettes/zucchini for this recipe. They have deep ridges along their length and they are skinnier and drier than ordinary courgettes. They are crunchy rather than juicy, and intensely flavoured. You can grow them from seed (Franchi Seeds of Italy) very successfully in this country. I hope you might have a go.

150 ml/$\frac{2}{3}$ cup olive oil
1 kg/2 lb. 4 oz. courgettes/zucchini,
   cut into thin slices
500 g/1 lb. 2 oz. bucatini pasta
55 g/3$\frac{1}{2}$ tablespoons unsalted butter,
   cut into little pieces
115 g/1$\frac{1}{2}$ cups freshly grated Parmesan
115 g/4 oz. freshly grated sweet
   Provolone cheese
handful of fresh mint and basil,
   freshly torn
sea salt and freshly ground
   black pepper

Serves 6

Heat the oil in a large deep frying pan/skillet and fry a few courgette slices at a time for about 3 minutes until golden. Remove and place in a large bowl.

Cook the pasta in a large pan of boiling salted water until al dente. This will very much depend on personal preference, so taste as you are cooking and stop when the pasta is cooked to your liking. Drain, reserving a cup of pasta water, return the pasta to the pan and add the fried courgettes as well as the butter, cheeses, herbs, salt and pepper. Mix well to form an emulsion, adding some of the reserved pasta cooking water if needed. Serve immediately.

SPAGHETTI WITH LEMON & CREAM
SPAGHETTI AL LIMONE

This is an iconic dish from the Amalfi coast, with at least a thousand different variations - in essence though, just 5 ingredients and only 15 minutes to prepare.

600 g/1 lb. 5 oz. spaghetti
300 ml/1$\frac{1}{4}$ cups double/heavy cream
freshly squeezed juice of 1 lemon
grated zest of 3 lemons
90 g/$\frac{1}{3}$ cup unsalted butter, at room
   temperature
sea salt and freshly ground
   black pepper

Serves 6

Boil the pasta in a large pan of boiling, salted water (only salt the water when the water starts to boil) and cook until al dente. This will very much depend on personal preference, so taste as you are cooking and stop when the pasta is cooked to your liking.

Drain the pasta, reserving 240 ml/1 cup of the cooking water. Add the cream, lemon juice, zest and butter and mix very well indeed. Add some of the reserved pasta cooking water to slacken the sauce if needed. Season to taste and enjoy straightaway.

GNOCCHI WITH RICOTTA
RICOTTA GNOCCHI 'NDUNDERI'

This dish is truly Minorese and is made to celebrate the feast of the patron saint of the village Santa Trofimena on 13 July. I've been extremely fortunate to have made them for Sky Italia with Gennaro Contaldo, a magnificent, kind and talented chef, also from Minori. He remembers many of my relatives, long since departed, so it is always so comforting to meet up with him and reminisce.

300 g/10½ oz. ricotta cheese, drained
125 g/scant 1 cup Italian '00' flour, plus extra for dusting
40 g/½ cup freshly grated Parmesan cheese, plus extra to serve
2 large/US extra-large egg yolks
1 teaspoon freshly grated nutmeg
sea salt and freshly ground black pepper

SAUCE
2 tablespoons olive oil
350 g/12 oz. cherry tomatoes on the vine, halved
2 garlic cloves, finely chopped
12 fresh basil leaves, roughly torn
2 tablespoons good-quality extra virgin olive oil
pinch of dried chillies/chiles (*peperoncino*) (optional)

ridged gnocchi paddle (see Notes opposite)

Serves 6

For the gnocchi, mix all the ingredients together in a medium bowl. Turn the dough onto a lightly floured work surface and knead gently until smooth.

Roll the dough into long ropes, the thickness of your middle finger, then cut to form 2-cm/¾-in. short lengths. Roll these lengths on a ridged gnocchi paddle, place on a floured tray and refrigerate until needed.

To make the sauce, heat the olive oil in a medium pan and add the tomatoes, garlic and a pinch of sea salt. Heat over a medium heat to encourage the tomatoes to become juicy and squashy. Cook for 6 minutes, then season and add the torn basil and extra virgin olive oil. Adjust the seasoning to your liking, sometimes you might like to add peperoncino.

Cook the gnocchi in a large pan of boiling salted water for at least 6-8 minutes; they will float to the top of the pan when ready.

Remove the gnocchi with a slotted spoon and stir them into the warmed sauce. Add a little gnocchi cooking water to the sauce to create an emulsion. Mix well and serve immediately with plenty of freshly grated Parmesan cheese.

NOTES:
• *Always smell cherry tomatoes on the vine to ensure they have a good peppery aroma.*

• *You may like to add some peperoncino (hot chilli peppers) to the sauce for an extra kick.*

• *If you don't have a ridged gnocchi paddle, you can also create the same indentations using the tines of a fork or by gently pressing each gnocchi over a sushi matt.*

SPAGHETTI WITH FISH SAUCE
COLATURA DI ALICI

Colatura is available online these days from Sous Chef and other good delis. It is a delicious sauce, made by fermenting anchovies and other fish. The fish juices are then strained and the result is *colatura*; it's amazing.

80 g/1 cup dried breadcrumbs
75 ml/5 tablespoons good-quality extra
   virgin olive oil
450 g/1 lb. dried spaghetti
3 tablespoons *colatura* (Italian fish sauce)
1 garlic clove, grated
1 teaspoon dried chilli/chile flakes
   (*peperoncino*)
20 g/³⁄₄ oz. fresh flat-leaf parsley,
   chopped
2 teaspoons finely grated lemon zest
freshly squeezed juice of 1 lemon
sea salt and freshly ground black pepper

Serves 4

In a small frying pan/skillet, combine the breadcrumbs and 1 tablespoon of the olive oil and cook over a medium heat, stirring constantly, until toasted and golden. Season with salt and pepper and leave to one side.

Cook the pasta in in a large pan of boiling, salted water until al dente. This will very much depend on personal preference, so taste as you are cooking and stop when the pasta is cooked to your liking.

Meanwhile, combine the colatura, garlic and peperoncino in a bowl and mix well with 2 tablespoons of pasta water to form an emulsion. Add the remaining oil.

Drain the pasta, reserving a cup of the cooking water, and add the colatura mixture, mixing vigorously. Add the breadcrumbs, parsley, lemon zest and juice. Taste and add more colatura if necessary and some of the reserved pasta cooking water to slacken the sauce if needed. Eat immediately.

THIN PASTA WITH SPICY TOMATO SAUCE
TAGLIONI ALLA PUTTANESCA

Invented in Naples in the mid 20th century, this is a tremendous combination of flavours. Spicy, fruity and salty, and always so good after a long day sailing, swimming and just being by the water's edge.

500 g/1 lb. 2 oz. taglioni pasta
100 ml/generous ¹⁄₃ cup olive oil
2 garlic cloves, crushed
generous pinch of dried chilli/chile flakes
   (*peperoncino*)
8 anchovy fillets, drained and soaked
   in milk for 30 minutes
400-g/14-oz. can good-quality plum
   tomatoes
100 g/3¹⁄₂ oz. black olives in oil, stoned/
   pitted and chopped
15 g/1¹⁄₂ tablespoons capers
handful of fresh oregano
handful of fresh flat-leaf parsley, chopped

Serves 6

Cook the pasta in a large pan of salted boiling water until al dente. This will very much depend on personal preference, so taste as you are cooking and stop when the pasta is cooked to your liking. Drain the pasta, reserving a cup of the cooking water for later.

Meanwhile, heat the olive oil in a heavy-based saucepan and gently fry the garlic and chilli without browning. Drain the anchovies and add to the pan, mashing them up while stirring.

Add the tomatoes, olives, capers, oregano and parsley (reserving a little to garnish) and cook over a medium heat, stirring occasionally, for 10 minutes. Add the drained pasta to the sauce and mix very well together. Add some or the reserved pasta cooking water to slacken the sauce if needed.

Serve immediately with the reserved oregano and parsley sprinkled over.

CHICKPEA PASTA WITH SQUID & CHICKPEAS
LAGANELLE CON CALAMARI E CECI

I've experimented extensively with this recipe and found that using this ratio of chickpea/gram flour to '00' flour gives a great flavour and makes the dough easy handle. This is one of my all-time favourite recipes in this book.

175 g/1⅓ cups chickpea/gram flour
480 g/3⅔ cups Italian '00' flour
6 large/US extra-large eggs
semolina, for dusting

SAUCE
60 ml/¼ cup olive oil
3 garlic cloves, sliced
1–2 small hot chillies/chiles
1 kg/2 lb. 4 oz. small, whole squid, cleaned and cut into 1-cm/½-in. thick rings, tentacles left whole
60 ml/¼ cup dry white wine
450 g/1 lb. ripe cherry tomatoes on the vine, cut in half
300 g/2 cups cooked chickpeas/ garbanzos, drained if necessary
very generous handful of fresh flat-leaf parsley, chopped
sea salt and freshly ground black pepper

Serves 6

Mix the flours together well. Make a well in the centre and add the eggs. Mix the eggs well with a fork (only the egg, not yet drawing in the flour). Once the eggs are slack, glide in the flour to create a paste. Knead well so that a strong but soft clump is formed that is as smooth as marble.

Rest the dough in the fridge for 10-15 minutes, depending on the temperature in your kitchen. Divide the dough into 3 equal portions. Keep the pieces that you are not working with covered with a clean kitchen cloth.

Roll the sections through a pasta machine one at a time. Roll the sheets just before the last setting. Using a fluted pastry wheel cut each sheet into 18-cm/7-in.lengths and arrange on a clean kitchen cloth dusted with semolina. Dry the pasta slightly, turning the sheets occasionally – the surface of the pasta should be dry to the touch but flexible. Attach the cutting blade to the pasta machine. Pass each sheet of dough through the wide cutting blade. Transfer to a kitchen cloth and dust with semolina.

Bring a very large pan of well salted water to the boil. Stir in the pasta and cook for 3-5 minutes.

While the pasta is cooking make the sauce. Heat the olive oil in a pan big enough to hold the pasta and sauté the garlic and chilli. Add the prepared squid and cook over a medium-high heat for 1 minute. Pour in the wine and simmer briskly. Add the tomatoes, chickpeas and half the parsley. Pour in 125 ml/½ cup of the pasta cooking water and simmer for 1 minute. Season well with salt and pepper and combine with the drained pasta. Avoid cooking the squid for longer than 5 minutes to avoid it becoming rubbery. Add more parsley and serve immediately.

GREEN CHICORY RAVIOLI
RAVIOLI CON CICORIA

We Italians just love our greens. As a filling for ravioli, the slightly bitter *cicoria* (chicory/endive) leaves provide a perfect foil for the sweeter tomato sauce, but you could use spinach, Swiss chard or rocket/arugula instead. I first enjoyed this dish in Venice in a little café on a very cold day in February before the Carnival. I went back for dinner and had the same dish again, just so that I could commit the flavour to memory.

PASTA
115 g/generous ¾ cup Italian '00' flour
115 g/generous ¾ cup semolina flour
2 eggs (the largest you can find)
sea salt

FILLING
500 g/1 lb. 2 oz. chicory/endive leaves, trimmed
250 g/9 oz. ricotta cheese, fresh if possible (or tub ricotta)
1 garlic clove, crushed
pinch of dried chilli/chile flakes (*peperoncino*), to taste
1 egg (the largest you can find)
100 g/1⅓ cups freshly grated Parmesan
sea salt and freshly ground black pepper

TO SERVE
55 g/3½ tablespoons unsalted butter
Puttanesca Sauce (see page 67), warmed
freshly grated Parmesan

Serves 4

Make the pasta as described on page 70. Roll as described, then cut into 7.5-cm/3-in. wide strips.

To start the stuffing, boil the chicory in a pan of salted water for 7–10 minutes until tender, then drain well and finely chop.

Mix together the ricotta, garlic, dried chilli flakes, egg and Parmesan, with salt and pepper to taste. Make little balls and put them on a pasta strip, about 7.5 cm/3 in. apart. Cover with another pasta strip, and use a ravioli cutter to seal and cut out the filled ravioli. Continue until all the dough and filling are used up. You now have a window of opportunity of around 1½ hours to cook and use the ravioli before the filling starts to seep through the pasta.

Simmer the ravioli in a large pan of salted water for about 8 minutes, or until they bob to the top of the water. Drain and serve with the butter, warmed Puttanesca sauce and Parmesan.

HANDMADE FUSILLI WITH TOMATO & CLAMS
FUSILLI DIVINA

The divine coast is how many famous poets referred to the splendour of Amalfi. The shape and curling of fusilli is unique to this region and is worthwhile mastering how to make. I have happily given instructions on how to make this pasta shape in many of my workshops. It can be tricky, so might take a bit of practice to master.

420 g/scant 3¼ cups Italian '00' flour, plus extra for dusting
pinch of sea salt

SAUCE
1 kg/2 lb. 4 oz. clams
1 tablespoon Italian '00' flour, plus extra for dusting
2 tablespoons capers, chopped
2 garlic cloves, sliced
125 ml/½ cup olive oil
600 g/1 lb. 5 oz. plum tomatoes, cored, seeded and cut into 2-cm/¾-in. chunks
handful of fresh flat-leaf parsley, chopped
200 g/7 oz. rocket/arugula
sea salt and freshly ground black pepper

bamboo skewer or thin metal rod

Serves 6

To make the pasta, tip the flour onto a wooden board. Mix 250 ml/1 cup water and the salt together. Make a well in the flour and gradually add the water. Using a fork, work the water into the flour, bit by bit, to form a strong, soft dough. Knead vigorously for at least 10 minutes to form a smooth dough. The dough will be supple and smooth, like marble. There might be leftover flour – this always depends on the flour type, the temperature and where the flour has been stored. Cover the dough and leave to rest for 30 minutes.

Line 2 baking trays with clean kitchen cloths and dust lightly with some flour.

Cut off a small grape-sized piece of the dough, keeping the unused portion of dough wrapped well while you work. Roll the small piece of dough by hand on a wooden board into a 6-mm/¼-in. thick rope. Cut the rope into 5.5-cm/2¼-in. pieces. To make the spiral shape, dust each piece of dough with flour and curl one end around a bamboo skewer or thin metal rod. Hold it in place and rest the skewer on the board. Roll it away from you. The pasta will wrap itself around the skewer like a coil. To thin the coil, hold it in place with 2 hands and roll the skewer back and forth while gently stretching the coil outwards. The finished fusilli should be 5.5 cm/2¼ in. long. Transfer to the cloth-lined trays for the pasta to dry for a few minutes.

To make the sauce, place the clams in a large bowl filled with cold water. Stir in the flour and soak for 15 minutes. Lift them out of the water and soak in clear water for 10 minutes, then drain the clams.

Cook the fusilli in a large pan of boiling salted water for 3–5 minutes. This will very much depend on personal preference, so taste as you are cooking and stop when the pasta is cooked to your liking.

Meanwhile, sauté the garlic in the olive oil in a large pan over a medium heat. Stir in the tomatoes, parsley and capers, increase the heat and add the clams and 250 ml/1 cup water from the pasta pot. Cook briskly, just until all the clams have opened (discard any clams that have not opened). Reserve a small amount of rocket/arugula for garnish and add the rest to the pot. Stir until wilted, and add seasoning to taste. Remove the sauce from the heat. Drain the fusilli, add to the clams and mix well. Garnish with the reserved rocket.

HANDMADE BASIL PASTA WITH AUBERGINE & TOMATO
SCIALATELLI CON MELANZANE E POMODORI

This particular recipe is from the famous Hotel Santa Caterino. It has been open to the public for 90 years and boasts some of the best food in the whole of Campania. The hotel has an enviable cliff position with amazing views and they have their own kitchen gardens, which makes for the most amazing food.

400 g/3 cups Italian '00' flour, plus extra for dredging
375 ml/generous 1½ cups whole milk
1 large/US extra-large egg
60 g/¾ cup finely grated Parmesan, plus extra to serve
2½ teaspoons finely chopped fresh basil leaves, plus extra to serve
1 medium aubergine/eggplant, sliced into 1.25-cm/½-in. thick pieces
60 ml/¼ cup olive oil
3 garlic cloves, thinly sliced
3 medium tomatoes, cut into 1.25-cm/½-in. chunks
150 g/5½ oz. mozzarella, cut into 1-cm/½-in. dice
sea salt

Serves 6

To make the pasta dough, tip the flour onto a wooden board, make a well in the centre and add the milk, egg, Parmesan and finely chopped basil. Mix thoroughly, using a fork to make a ball of dough. Knead using your hands so that the dough is strong and soft like silk. Cover and rest in the fridge for 30 minutes.

Meanwhile, layer the aubergine/eggplant in a colander, salting each layer. Rest a heavy weight on the aubergine and leave for about 20 minutes. Then rinse off the salt and dry the aubergine with paper towels. Cut into 1.25-cm/½-in. dice and set aside.

Now roll the pasta, either by hand (my preferred method) or through a pasta machine. If using a pasta machine, cut the dough into quarters so that you are only working with a quarter at a time, whilst keeping the remaining dough covered.

Laminate the dough by putting it through the machine at the highest setting. Fold the dough a quarter turn and make into an envelope shape. Do this twice and work through the settings, stopping at the setting before the last. Lay the pasta out onto a floured surface and leave to become drier before cutting into tagliatelle. Continue with the remaining quarters of the pasta dough.

Returning to the aubergine, heat half of the oil in a large frying pan/skillet. Dredge the aubergine with flour and fry over a medium-high heat to colour the aubergine. Remove from the pan.

Cook the pasta in a large pan of salted boiling water until al dente. This will very much depend on personal preference, so taste as you are cooking and stop when the pasta is cooked to your liking. Drain the pasta, reserving a cup of the cooking water.

Meanwhile, heat the remaining oil in a large pan over a medium heat. Add the garlic and cook gently before adding the tomatoes, shredded basil and aubergine. Add a little of the reserved pasta cooking water to slacken the sauce if needed. Add the cooked pasta to the pan and stir through so that it is coated in the sauce. Serve scattered with the mozzarella, basil leaves and extra Parmesan.

SPAGHETTI WITH LOBSTER SAUCE
SPAGHETTI CON SALSA DI ARAGOSTINE

The best lobsters are tiny and sweet and are found on the Amalfi coast. The richness of their flavour contrasts wonderfully with the simplicity of the spaghetti. Twirl the pasta in the usual way, but dive in with your hands as well - something the Italians love to do.

3 small live lobsters or lobster tails, weighing about 400 g/14 oz. each
3 tablespoons olive oil
2 garlic cloves, chopped
generous pinch of dried chilli/chile flakes (peperoncino)
125 ml/½ cup dry white wine
handful of fresh flat-leaf parsley, roughly chopped
350 g/12 oz. spaghetti
2 tablespoons good-quality extra virgin olive oil, for drizzling
sea salt and freshly ground black pepper

Serves 4

Bring a large pan of salted water to the boil and drop in the lobsters. Simmer for 12 minutes, then drain and leave to cool. Halve the lobsters and remove the flesh from the bodies, discarding the stomach sacs.

Crack the pincers and remove the meat. Keep to one side.

Heat the olive oil in a large sauté pan, add the garlic and dried chilli. Sauté for a couple of minutes, then add the wine. Bring to the boil, add the cooked lobster meat and the parsley and simmer for 4 more minutes. Season with salt and pepper.

Cook the spaghetti in a pan of boiling salted water until al dente. This will very much depend on personal preference, so taste as you are cooking and stop when the pasta is cooked to your liking. Drain, reserving a cup of cooking water.

Toss the spaghetti with the lobster sauce, adding a little of the pasta cooking water to slacken the sauce if needed. Drizzle with extra virgin olive oil and serve at once.

SPAGHETTI FROM CAPRI
SPAGHETTI ALLA CAPRESE

Caprese means 'in the style of Capri'. A blissfully simple idea for a scorching hot day, this is refreshingly light and provides oceans of energy. Fuss free and made in moments. Always remember, please use the finest ingredients wherever possible.

250 g/9 oz. cherry tomatoes on the vine, ripe and flavourful (or datterini tomatoes, if available), cut into quarters
1 garlic clove, sliced
45 ml/3 tablespoons olive oil
500 g/1 lb. 2 oz. spaghetti
125 g/4½ oz. buffalo mozzarella, torn into bite-sized pieces
generous handful of fresh basil, torn
2 teaspoons chopped fresh oregano
sea salt and freshly ground black pepper
freshly grated Parmesan, to serve

Serves 4-6

Place the tomatoes in a large bowl with the garlic, oil and salt and leave to marinate for 30 minutes.

Meanwhile, cook the spaghetti in a large pan of boiling, salted water until al dente. This will very much depend on personal preference, so taste as you are cooking and stop when the pasta is cooked to your liking. Drain, reserving a cup of cooking water.

Add the mozzarella to the marinating tomatoes. Add the spaghetti to the bowl of tomatoes and mix through, adding a little of the pasta cooking water if needed. Sprinkle with basil and oregano. Serve straight away, sprinkled with Parmesan.

MAIN PLATES
PIATTI PRINCIPALI

THE MAIN EVENT

Cooking on the Amalfi Coast is dictated by the area's geography, climate and ingredients. Because it is coastal, most courses in a meal – and particularly the *piatto principale* or 'main plate' – are dominated by the multifarious fruits of the sea: fish, shellfish and cephalopods such as squid. I will never tire of going to the beach, wherever I am in the world, and buying fish for lunch or supper from the fishermen is a big part of that. The quality is superb and does not need much elaboration in its cooking.

The fishermen of the Amalfi Coast are famed for their bravery, going out on the fickle sea every day, not quite knowing what to expect from the weather. (Their wives are just as brave, left waiting on the shore.) Storms in this area are breathtaking, seeming to come from nowhere, in July and August mostly. Stanley Tucci filmed one such Amalfi Coast storm in his recent television series – but the feast they enjoyed in the restaurant more than made up for the vagaries of the weather! I remember stormy waves reaching the balconies of our house on the seafront in Minori, sweeping pots of basil and geraniums from one side to the other. These storms are sometimes a relief from the relentless midsummer heat – which we call *Lucifero* (Lucifer, or the devil) – as if nature had decided that it needed to cool everything down with a storm. The aquifers, plants and animals are grateful, too!

Fish is the prime ingredient of main courses served in homes and restaurants on the Amalfi Coast and will depend on what has been brought in by the fishermen that day. In the summer, with warmer weather, the fish are more plentiful. They are cooked quickly and simply, often with nothing more than a halved Amalfi lemon as accompaniment, or a drizzle of extra virgin olive oil. Tuna might be marinated first and the tender flesh of some fish could benefit from a wrapping of thin slices of courgette/zucchini. Salads are very characteristic of the area and both squid and octopus contribute masses of flavour (the combination of octopus or squid with potatoes is a speciality of Praiano). Small fish, such as anchovies, squid and prawns would be coated in a light batter, deep-fried and served with lemon. You might encounter similar on the street, offered in a paper cone (*cuoppo*) with a toothpick and lemon wedge.

In winter, the choice of seafood is not perhaps so wide, but I love the fact that eating in Italy and the Amalfi Coast is still dictated by the seasons; we enjoy one season, and then move on to another. In the UK and elsewhere, the idea of seasonal eating has been lost, with so many ingredients coming in from all over the world at all times of the year.

Very little meat is eaten domestically along the Amalfi Coast. Obviously, the restaurants will have to offer a choice – steaks for the tourists, say – but at home, apart from *salame* and other cured meats – meat was, and is, considered a luxury item, for high days and holidays only. Again, geography plays a part in this, as the Amalfi Coast, with its craggy, vertiginous terraces, has little grazing land for sheep, goats or cows. Any meat that is on offer would come from inland or from other nearby regions – lamb, for instance, would come from Calabria, where it is popular. Beef and veal are seen occasionally: perhaps a *nonna* (grandmother) might prepare a *ragù napolitana* on a Sunday. Rolls of thinly sliced beef or veal encasing a tasty filling, or chunks of meat, would be cooked for several hours in a tomato and wine sauce; this sauce, enriched by its meaty absorption, would dress the pasta course, and then the meat would be eaten as the *piatto principale* with a vegetable or, usually, alone.

Chickens mostly come from the farms above the Amalfi Coast, as there is not enough room for them nearer the sea. But they will be corn-fed, plump, yellow in colour and delicious. Rabbits might be reared domestically – they don't take up much space. Game birds are occasionally found on Amalfi Coast menus, shot by local hunters, as is wild rabbit.

There are few main-course ingredients in the culinary palette of the Amalfi Coast. The choice is limited, the cooking is simple and the quality of each ingredient is paramount. As a teacher of cooking, I tell my students always to try and buy less but better, whether meat, chicken or fish – it will be more expensive, but the taste will be superb. And if you eat less of an expensive chicken, say, at one meal, you will have leftovers for another meal. Also, because you won't serve that expensive meat or fish very often – echoing the Italian way – the dish will inevitably be that much more memorable!

STEAMED FRUITS OF THE SEA
FRUTTI DI MARE IN UMIDO

One of the primary wonders of seafood is that it is so quick and simple, utterly divine and very nutritious; these are facts long known to us in Italy. This recipe is a perfect example of this. When it is scorching hot in Italy, we do not want to be slaving away in the kitchen.

24 mussels
24 clams (Venus clams if possible)
4-6 slices of dry white country bread
60 ml/¼ cup olive oil
2 garlic cloves, crushed
2 plum tomatoes, deseeded and chopped
handful of fresh flat-leaf parsley
350 ml/1½ cups dry white wine

Serves 4-6

Preheat the oven to 180°C fan/200°C/400°F/gas 6.

Prepare the shellfish. Remove the beards from the mussels and scrub the shells. Wash the clams thoroughly and discard any clams or mussels that do not close.

Arrange the bread slices in a single layer on a baking sheet and toast in the preheated oven for 6 minutes. Turn the slices over and toast for 6 more minutes. Leave to cool on a wire rack.

Heat the oil in a large sauté pan over a medium heat. Add the garlic and cook gently until the garlic has softened. Add the tomatoes and half the parsley, increase the heat to medium-high and cook, stirring constantly for 1 minute.

Pour in the wine and simmer briskly until the wine has evaporated. Add the mussels and clams and reduce the heat to medium. Cover the pan and cook for 10 minutes, shaking the pan intermittently until all the shells have opened. Discard any that have remained closed.

Transfer the seafood to a long serving platter. Scatter with the remaining parsley and arrange the toasted bread around the edge of the platter. Serve immediately.

SPAGHETTI WITH CLAMS
SPAGHETTI ALLE VONGOLE

There would be an outcry in my family if this recipe was not included. Finest quality always please, although do not use fresh spaghetti in this recipe, and always check on the label that the spaghetti is made with durum wheat.

1 kg/2 lb. 4 oz. clams
500 g/1 lb. 2 oz. spaghetti
125 ml/½ cup good-quality extra
   virgin olive oil
2 garlic cloves, chopped
3 tablespoons chopped fresh flat-leaf
   parsley
2 teaspoons dried chilli/chile flakes
   (peperoncino)
sea salt

Serves 6

Place the clams in a large bowl, cover with salt water and leave for at least 30 minutes (longer if possible) to clean them.

Cook the pasta in a large pan of boiling salted water until al dente. This will very much depend on personal preference, so taste as you are cooking and stop when the pasta is cooked to your liking. Drain, reserving a cup of cooking water.

Heat the oil in a large frying pan/skillet over a medium heat, add the garlic and fry for a minute. Add the cleaned clams with the parsley and dried chillies. Cook for about 5 minutes until all the clams are open, discarding any that are still closed, and serve hot with the pasta, adding a little of the pasta cooking water if needed to slacken the sauce.

SPICY SQUID SALAD
PICCANTE INSALATA DI CALAMARI

When you are sitting at the table, looking out to sea after messing about on a boat most of the day and swimming in the sea, with the sun setting and the air sweet and aromatic, this dish is paradise.

1 baby cos lettuce, washed and dried
1 kg/2 lb. 4 oz. squid, cleaned, scored on
   the inside and cut into strips
30 ml/2 tablespoons olive oil
½ red onion, thinly sliced
20 g/¾ oz. fresh mint leaves
20 g/¾ oz. fresh basil leaves
1 red chilli/chile, seeded and thinly sliced

DRESSING
2 garlic cloves
1 small red chilli/chile, roughly chopped
1 teaspoon sea salt
30 ml/2 tablespoons fresh lemon juice
grated zest of 1 lemon
30 ml/2 tablespoons olive oil

Serves 6

Arrange the lettuce leaves on a large serving plate or 6 individual plates.

Place all the dressing ingredients into a food processor or blender and blend until smooth.

Place the squid and olive oil in a bowl and mix well. Preheat a large frying pan/skillet over a medium heat until hot and cook the squid for 1-2 minutes on each side, or until just cooked. Take care not to overcook the squid or it will be tough.

Transfer the cooked squid to a large bowl and add the onion, mint, basil and chilli. Pour over the dressing and toss to combine. Pile the dressed squid on top of the lettuce leaves to serve.

FISH WRAPPED IN COURGETTE FLOWERS
PESCI SERRA AI FIORI DI ZUCCA

This is a recipe for late spring, early summer. It is bright in colour, very dramatic when presented at the table and full of simple good flavours. Courgette/zucchini blossoms should be available to buy at your local greengrocer or better still, grow them yourself if you can.

8 medium courgettes/zucchini, trimmed
675 g /1$\frac{1}{2}$ lb. swordfish steaks, 2.5 cm/1 in. thick, skin removed (or tuna)
24 courgette/zucchini blossoms
1 large egg, beaten
60 ml/$\frac{1}{4}$ cup olive oil
2 garlic cloves, crushed
175 ml /$\frac{3}{4}$ cup dry white wine
sea salt and freshly ground black pepper

Serves 6

Slice half the courgettes lengthwise, 2 mm thick, using a large chef's knife. You should have 24 slices. Grate the remaining courgettes.

Fill a large pan with water, bring to the boil and add salt. Blanch the courgette slices in the boiling water for 2 minutes, or until flexible.

Cut the fish into 24 pieces about 6 cm/2$\frac{1}{4}$ in. long and 1 cm/$\frac{1}{2}$ in. wide and season with salt and pepper.

Ease the courgette blossoms open and remove the stamens. Rinse them under cold water and pat dry with paper towels. Brush the inside of each with beaten egg and wrap it lengthways around a piece of fish.

Heat the olive oil in a large sauté pan over a medium heat. Add the grated courgette, garlic and wine and boil briskly for 2 minutes. Season with salt and pepper.

Wrap a slice of blanched courgette around the centre of each piece of fish, then arrange the fish parcels on top of the shredded courgette in the pan. Cover the pan and cook for 7-10 minutes, or until the fish is cooked.

MARINATED TUNA
TEGLIA DI TONNO

When truly fresh, this dish is awesomely good. The fish is often cooked on the *brace*
(on the barbecue/grill) and served with lemon capers.

6 tuna steaks (about 175 g/6 oz. each)
250 ml/1 cup dry white wine
1 fresh rosemary sprig, leaves removed
   and finely chopped
4 garlic cloves, finely chopped
handful of fresh mint leaves, chopped
100 g/3½ oz. fine dried breadcrumbs
3 tablespoons capers, chopped
4 tablespoons olive oil
juice of 1 lemon
sea salt and freshly ground black pepper

Serves 6

Place the tuna steaks in a bowl and season with salt and pepper. Pour over the wine and add the chopped rosemary, garlic and mint. Turn, so that all of the tuna steaks are coated and leave to marinate for at least an hour.

Mix the breadcrumbs together with the capers in a small bowl. Drain the fish, reserving the marinade.

Brush a large frying pan/skillet with a little of the oil and heat it over a medium heat. Sprinkle the tuna steaks with the breadcrumbs and capers. Add the steaks, two or three at a time, to the hot pan and cook on both sides until nearly cooked through, basting with the marinade as you cook. This should take about 8 minutes altogether.

Whisk the rest of the oil with the lemon juice in a small bowl. Pour over the fish and cook for a few minutes more - this keeps the fish tender. Serve immediately.

SCALLOPS WITH LEMON, BAY LEAVES & ROSEMARY OIL
CAPESANTE CON LIMONE, ALLORO E OLIO DI ROSMARINO

This recipe is so simple that it hardly needs a method. It's from the Naples area, where many of the
best fish and shellfish recipes are to be found. Rosemary - used here as a skewer - grows in profusion
all over Italy and enhances fish dishes wonderfully.

2 unwaxed lemons
12 fat, fresh scallops, coral removed
   (which can be frozen and kept for
   stock)
4 tough rosemary stalks, leaves removed
   and retained
12 fresh bay leaves
1½ tablespoons olive oil
sea salt and freshly ground black pepper

Serves 4

Preheat the oven to 180°C fan/200°C/400°F/gas 6.

Pare the zest from the lemons and cut into 12 pieces.

Thread 3 scallops onto each rosemary stalk, alternating with 3 pieces of lemon zest and 3 bay leaves.

Pound the rosemary leaves and oil together in a mortar and pestle until fine, then pour this over the scallops. Squeeze over the lemon juice and leave to marinate for 20 minutes.

Place the rosemary and scallop skewers in a roasting tin and season well. Bake in the preheated oven for 8 minutes until the scallops are no longer opaque and have a nutty brown coating.

GRILLED FISH WITH MINT SAUCE
PESCE ALLA GRIGLIA CON SABA DE MENTE

I make no apologies for the use of mint in this book – it grows extensively along the Amalfi Coast and works miracles with fish and also vegetables. I grow copious amounts in my own garden for this very reason.

1 whole sea bass or red
   snapper, scaled and gutted
1 garlic clove, chopped
1 tablespoon chopped fresh
   flat-leaf parsley
1 tablespoon chopped fresh
   mint
45 ml/3 tablespoons olive oil
2 teaspoons Italian '00' flour
sea salt and freshly ground
   black pepper

MINT SAUCE
185 ml/¾ cup good-quality
   extra virgin olive oil
1 garlic clove, finely chopped
2 tablespoons white wine
   vinegar
3 tablespoons fresh lemon
   juice
very generous handful of
   chopped fresh mint

Serves 4

To make the mint sauce, mix the oil, garlic, vinegar, lemon juice and salt in a medium bowl. Mix with a whisk, then stir in the mint. Leave to infuse for 1 hour for maximum flavour.

Preheat the grill/broiler.

Rinse the fish, pat dry and season the cavity with salt. Combine the garlic, parsley, mint and oil in a small bowl, then rub the mixture over the fish. Season the fish with salt and dust with some of the flour.

Grill/broil the fish for 8-10 minutes. Turn the fish using a large metal spatula. Sprinkle with salt and flour and grill for a further 8-10 minutes on the other side. To test for doneness, insert a small paring knife into the fleshiest part of the fish; it should be flaky and opaque.

Transfer the fish to a large serving platter and serve with the tasty mint sauce.

BABY OCTOPUS & POTATO SALAD
POLPETTI E PATATE

With my father having been a potato grower and farmer, potatoes have always been a big part of my life. I love them and find this recipe is hard to beat when you are looking for something that is both light and satisfying.

3 fresh bay leaves
1 teaspoon black peppercorns
850 g/1 lb. 14 oz. baby octopus, cleaned (see Note below)
50 ml/3 tablespoons good-quality extra virgin olive oil
500 g/1 lb. 2 oz. new potatoes, peeled and cut into even sizes
1 celery stick, thinly sliced
juice and zest of 1 unwaxed lemon
handful of fresh flat-leaf parsley, chopped
sea salt and freshly ground black pepper

Serves 4-6

Fill a large pan with water, add the bay leaves and peppercorns and bring to the boil. Add the octopus, cover and cook for 15 minutes until it changes colour and has lovely tinges of pink – this may take longer or shorter, depending on the size of the octopus. Drain and discard the aromatics.

Heat 1 tablespoon of the olive oil in a large frying pan/skillet. Add the octopus and sauté for 3-5 minutes so that the skin blisters. Set aside.

Meanwhile, boil the potatoes in a large saucepan until tender when pierced with a knife, then drain. Arrange the potatoes on a serving platter with the octopus. Scatter over the celery and lemon zest, drizzle with the remaining oil and lemon juice and season with salt and pepper. Sprinkle with parsley and serve.

NOTE: *Clean the octopus yourself by removing the beak, eyes, internal cartilage and all the insides from the head. Wash well under cold running water and pat dry before use. (I usually ask my fishmonger to do this for me.)*

NONNA FERRIGNO'S CHICKEN CASSEROLE
POLLO ALLA CACCIATORE

This recipe is revisited so frequently in my home, not just for its taste, but also for its ease of cooking.
It is tasty, satisfying and also a one-pot meal, which is very useful for people short on time. I have experimented
over the years with various combinations, sometimes using smoky bacon, lardons or pancetta.
All of these are good additions.

2 tablespoons Italian '00' flour
8 chicken thighs, bone and skin
   on or off, depending on
   preference
45 ml/3 tablespoons olive oil
2 celery sticks, finely chopped
1 carrot, diced
1 red onion, diced
150 g/2½ cups chestnut
   mushrooms, coarsely
   chopped
1 garlic clove, crushed
45 ml/3 tablespoons white
   wine vinegar
2 fresh rosemary sprigs, leaves
   finely chopped
1 teaspoon fresh oregano
3 fresh bay leaves (or 2 dried)
90 ml/⅓ cup Italian passata
6 potatoes, peeled and
   quartered
handful of fresh flat-leaf
   parsley, chopped
sea salt and freshly ground
   black pepper

Serves 8

Put the flour on a plate and season with salt and pepper. Add the chicken thighs and toss to coat evenly.

Set a flameproof casserole dish over a medium heat, add the olive oil and heat gently. Add the flour-dusted chicken, cook for 8–10 minutes until coloured all over, then remove from the casserole dish.

Add more oil to the casserole dish if necessary, then add the celery, carrot, onion, mushrooms and garlic and cook for 5 minutes until lightly golden. Return the chicken to the dish and add the vinegar, herbs, passata, potatoes and 500 ml/2 cups cold water. Season well with salt and pepper.

Simmer gently, covered, for 45 minutes, checking that the casserole is not drying up and stirring it periodically to avoid it catching on the bottom of the dish.

Serve the casserole spooned into soup plates, garnished with parsley and accompany with focaccia or crusty bread to mop up the juices – in Italy this is know as *fare la scarpetta*.

STUFFED CHICKEN ROLLS
INVOLTINI DI POLLO

Veal is the most commonly consumed meat in Italy, in both the north and the south, and would traditionally be used for this recipe. This version using chicken is such a delightful dish - a Ferrigno family recipe. The smell transports me instantly to Minori.

60 g/2 oz. mozzarella
45 g/1½ oz. sliced prosciutto
6 whole skinless, boneless
   chicken breasts, halved
   and flattened
80 ml/⅓ cup olive oil
Italian '00' flour, for dredging
250 ml/1 cup dry white wine
250 ml/1 cup chicken broth
sea salt and freshly ground
   black pepper

STUFFING
120 g/4½ oz. minced veal
2 eggs, lightly beaten
1 garlic clove, finely chopped
handful of finely chopped fresh
   flat-leaf parsley
45 g/½ cup freshly grated
   Parmesan
25 g/⅓ cup dried breadcrumbs

Serves 6

To make the stuffing, combine the veal, eggs, garlic, parsley, Parmesan and breadcrumbs in a bowl. Add salt and pepper and mix thoroughly.

Cut the mozzarella and prosciutto into 12 equal pieces and set aside.

Arrange the chicken breasts on a large chopping board. Mound equal amounts of the veal mixture onto the centre of each piece of chicken, top with two pieces each of mozzarella and prosciutto. Roll up the chicken, tuck in the ends to enclose the filling and fasten with a toothpick.

Heat the oil in a heavy sauté pan large enough to hold the involtini in one layer over a medium heat. When the oil is hot, lightly dredge the chicken in flour and add half of them to the pan. Brown on all sides, then transfer to a plate. Cook the remaining involtini in the same way.

Pour the white wine into the pan and bring to the boil. Cook the wine at a brisk simmer until it is reduced by half. Return the involtini to the pan and add the broth. Cover and simmer for 30 minutes, then season with salt and pepper.

Transfer the involtini to a serving plate and remove the toothpicks. Spoon over the sauce (it may be reduced if desired).

VEAL & PORK MEATBALLS
POLPETTI ALLA FERRIGNO

Meatballs are a family dish and are slightly celebratory in feel, possibly because they take quite a while to make, and you will occasionally find them on a trattoria menu. You must use the best possible meat and ask the butcher to mince it as finely as he can for that melt-in-the-mouth effect. Never use ordinary butcher's mince, as it is too coarse and fatty, and meatballs made with it will fall apart.

2–3 tablespoons olive oil
1 onion, peeled and finely
  chopped
2–3 tablespoons tomato purée/
  paste
½ teaspoon caster/superfine
  sugar

MEATBALLS
500 g/1 lb. 2 oz. minced veal
500 g/1 lb. 2 oz. minced pork
2 large/US extra-large eggs
handful of fresh flat-leaf
  parsley, chopped
125 g/4½ oz. Parmesan, grated
2 slices of stale bread, soaked
  in milk and squeezed dry
125 g/4½ oz. diced pancetta
sea salt and freshly ground
  black pepper

Serves 8

Mix all the meatball ingredients together in a large bowl, then use your hands to shape into about 24 even-sized balls. Flatten each one slightly into oval shapes, about 1 cm/½ in. thick.

Heat the olive oil in a large frying pan/skillet and fry the meatballs for about 6 minutes until well browned on each side. Transfer to a flameproof casserole dish.

Add the onion, tomato purée, sugar and 200 ml/7 fl oz. water to the pan that you cooked the meatballs in. Cook for 5–10 minutes, stirring, then season with salt and pepper.

Pour the sauce over the meatballs in the casserole and add enough water to almost cover them. Cover and simmer over a low heat for 1 hour until the sauce has thickened and reduced.

VEAL SCALOPPINE WITH PARSLEY CAPER SAUCE

SCALOPPINE AI CAPPERI

I totally understand why this is so enjoyed and is so incredibly popular throughout the Amalfi Coast; it is light
on the digestion and quick to cook. I can remember my father coming home saying *andiamo a mangiare* (let's go and eat) –
and it was this we ate. Veal is now ethically produced, so in short, this recipe is perfect.

12 wafer-thin veal scaloppine
(ask your butcher to prepare for you)
'00' flour, for dredging
8 tablespoons unsalted butter
1 tablespoon olive oil
3 tablespoons capers, rinsed and drained
generous handful of fresh flat-leaf
parsley, plus extra to garnish
3 tablespoons meat broth
1 tablespoon white wine vinegar
sea salt and freshly ground black pepper

Serves 6

Dredge the scaloppine in the flour.

Heat the butter and oil in a large heavy frying pan/skillet until foamy. Fry
the scaloppine for 6 minutes on each side until golden brown. Remove the
scallopine with a slotted spoon and keep warm while you continue cooking.

Increase the heat to high and add the capers, parsley and some salt and
pepper to the pan. Cook for 5 minutes, stirring gently. Pour in the broth
and the vinegar and cook for a further 5 minutes.

Return the scallopine to the pan, turning, so that both sides are coated in
the juices. Serve immediately with extra parsley to garnish.

VEAL FLAT STEAKS

POLPETTONE DI VITELLO

This recipe is for my sister Gina, who just loves this homemade dish, which changes
quite frequently according to whatever takes my fancy.

450 g/1 lb. minced veal
1 garlic clove, crushed
handful of fresh flat-leaf parsley, finely
chopped
1 tablespoon tomato purée/paste
1 large/US extra-large egg, beaten
4 medium slices of bread, crusts removed
75 ml/⅓ cup white wine
handful of fresh breadcrumbs
2 tablespoons olive oil
sea salt and freshly ground black pepper

Serves 6

Combine the veal, garlic, parsley, tomato purée and egg in a large bowl
and season to taste.

Put the bread in a separate bowl and pour over the wine. Leave for a few
minutes until the bread has softened. Add the softened bread to the meat
mixture, then beat everything together with a wooden spoon.

Shape the mixture into 6 flat steaks, then dip each one in breadcrumbs.

Heat the olive oil in a large frying pan/skillet and, when it is hot, brown
the steaks on each side. Cover the pan with a lid and cook for a further
7 minutes, or until the meat is cooked. Serve.

Recipe illustrated on page 2

SKEWERED LAMB PARCELS
BRACIOLETTINE

This is a variation of one of my grandmother's recipes – and is a great example of how meat is served in Italy, either in the *trattoria* or at home. The meat is prepared simply and should be of the finest quality.

900 g/2 lb. top round of leg
   of lamb, cut into 5 mm/
   1/8 in. slices
18 bay leaves (fresh are best)
2 onions, peeled and cut into
   18 small wedges
45 ml/3 tablespoons olive oil,
   plus extra for oiling
handful of fine breadcrumbs
sea salt and freshly ground
   black pepper

FILLING
60 ml/1/4 cup olive oil
1 onion, peeled and finely
   chopped
100 g/3 1/2 oz. pecorino cheese,
   cubed
100 g/3 1/2 oz. pancetta, cubed
55 g/2 oz. bread, cubed
handful of fresh flat-leaf
   parsley, chopped
1 large/US extra-large egg,
   beaten

12 thin metal skewers

Serves 6

To make the filling, heat the olive oil in a saucepan over a medium heat, then sauté the onion for 5–8 minutes until golden. Remove from the heat and leave to cool. Add the pecorino, pancetta, bread, parsley and egg and mix well. Season to taste with salt and black pepper and set aside.

Beat the slices of lamb to tenderize them, then cut the slices into 8 cm/3 in. squares. Put 1 tablespoon of filling on each slice of meat, positioned near a corner. Roll the corner of meat over the stuffing, tuck in the edges and roll it into a small sausage shape, about 4 cm/1 1/2 in. thick x 8 cm/3 in. long. Continue until all the meat rolls are done.

Preheat the oven to 180°C fan/200°C/400°F/gas 6.

Oil a baking sheet and sprinkle it with salt. Push 2 skewers through the side of a meat roll and add on a bay leaf and a wedge of onion. Repeat, alternating the meat, bay and onion, to fill each double-skewer with 3 meat rolls.

Pour the olive oil into a flat plate and put the breadcrumbs on a second plate. Dip each skewer in the oil and then in the breadcrumbs. Arrange the coated skewers in a roasting tin and roast in the preheated oven for 20 minutes, turning after 10 minutes, until golden.

VEGETABLES & PRESERVES

CONTORNI E CONSERVE

THE SUPPORTING ACT

Land in Italy, not just in the south, is still used mainly for growing ingredients, rather than for grazing food animals. As a result, the Italians have always been very much more interested in vegetables as a major part of their diet and have been more inventive with their vegetable recipes. Indeed, southern Italians love vegetables so much that the Neapolitans – before they were 'macaroni-eaters' (see page 54) – were known as *mangiafoglie*, 'leaf-eaters'!

Vegetables are considered so vital to Italians that they have been given their own course in the meal, the *contorno*. This word also means 'contour', and is one of the 'contours' of a traditional Italian meal – the *antipasti* is the appetizer, the pasta the sustenance, the meat or fish the protein element, then the *contorno* is the *digestivo*, which helps with the digestion of the meal.

The whole region of Campania is one of the bread baskets of Italy. It has been blessed with all the elements for growing vegetables and fruit of the highest quality: the nutrient-rich volcanic soil, courtesy of Mount Vesuvius, lots of bright sunshine and occasional rain. The vegetables Campania is most famed for include tomatoes, aubergines/eggplant, courgettes/zucchini, asparagus, broccoli, cauliflowers, bell peppers and chilli peppers. Thanks to the abundance of sunshine, many of these vegetables crop twice a year.

Aubergines appear in menus in many guises – *parmigiana di melanzana* is said to come from Sicily, but its combination of aubergines, tomatoes and mozzarella seems quintessentially Amalfitano to me! They are also stuffed and baked (an Arab influence) and stewed for use in pasta sauces. Courgettes, too, are used in many ways. One favourite of mine is *alla scapece*, in which they are thinly sliced, dried, fried until brown, then dressed with oil, vinegar, garlic and mint. Their flowers are scattered on pizzas or stuffed with ricotta and other flavourings before being deep-fried. And another speciality of the Amalfi Coast is *fritto misto*, small pieces of vegetables, battered and deep-fried, in much the same way as fish. Occasionally in autumn, you might see wild mushrooms on local menus.

Herbs are grown along the Amalfi Coast and contribute massively to the intense flavour of many

local dishes. Many of these grow in the wild – fennel lines roadsides and the edges of fields and terraces, and you could utilize both the leaves and the seeds (think of those glorious Italian fennel *salsicchie*, 'sausages'). Basil is omnipresent in the south, with pots of it adorning every balcony, its perfume permeating the air. Mint, surprisingly, is a common flavour of the Amalfi Coast. It was brought in by the North Africans, but is used a lot with fish, courgettes and tomatoes.

It is interesting that Campania has been so important in the popularization and cultivation of many vegetables in Italy. As it was such an important port in centuries past, many new vegetables – imported by ship from the East or the New World – would have appeared first in Naples. The tomato and aubergine (both from the same family) and peppers came from the Americas and, after a few years of suspicion, became popular and part of the local agriculture and diet (tomatoes and peppers adorning the local street food known as pizza). The San Marzano tomato, which is the star of the Campanian vegetable scene, is a much later cultivar of the tomato originally imported. Many more of the vegetables with which we are familiar today were developed horticulturally in Italy, among them broccoli, fennel, celery, peas and artichokes.

Many ways of preparing, cooking and preserving vegetables have originated in Campania as well. Apart from the *alla scapece* mentioned before, there are also *sott'olio* (preserved in oil), *sott'aceto* (preserved in vinegar) and *agrodolce* (which is a sour-sweet preserving method). Preserving is something all Italians do; if you have plenty of a crop, you will want to keep some of it for later, when fresh is not available. In traditional kitchens on the Amalfi Coast, this preserving might start in spring and continue throughout the year. The local gossip would all be about whose dried tomatoes were the juiciest, whose bottled aubergines would taste the best...

Olive trees are also grown on terraces in the Amalfi Coast, although not as much as lemons (see page 7). We had a few trees in Minori, from which we might get a litre of oil from 5 kg/11 lb. of olives. It was, and still is, a precious commodity, and it is one of my favourite ingredients. It is fascinating to think that nature even controls how we use and appreciate olive oil. A good extra virgin is enjoyed in the winter months, after its harvesting and pressing in and around November. It is then that we need that extra pungency. In summer, the olive oil has become milder, so that when used to dress lighter foods, such as vegetables and lettuces, it does not conflict with the fresh summer flavour.

A quick olive oil tip. Put a ramekin of a good olive oil in the fridge, where it will set. It can then be used as a spread on bread or toast, which is much healthier than butter!

BREAD, VEGETABLE & MOZZARELLA SALAD
CAPONATA DI NAPOLI

I'm a very passionate sourdough baker and once a week I will proudly make a loaf. It's taken some time to perfect, and I so appreciate the journey. Now I am content with what I can produce, so it is well worth perfecting. We Italians are frugal, so this is a perfect example of making use of sourdough or day-old country bread, never wasting a morsel. But please, please always use the finest raw ingredients for this recipe - sun-ripened tomatoes, fruity, zingy extra virgin olive oil and the freshest possible buffalo mozzarella.

250 g/9 oz. sourdough or firm
   textured country-style bread
4-6 ripe, fruity tomatoes,
   deseeded and diced
250 g/9 oz. buffalo mozzarella,
   torn
1 teaspoon good-quality dried
   oregano, preferably from
   a stem
zest and juice of ½ unwaxed lemon
100 ml/generous ⅓ cup extra
   virgin olive oil
generous handful of fresh large
   basil leaves, torn
sea salt and freshly ground
   black pepper

Serves 4-6

Simply tear the bread into chunks and place in a large bowl. Add the tomatoes, mozzarella, oregano, lemon zest and juice and season with salt and pepper. Drizzle generously with fabulous oil, mix gently and serve topped with torn basil leaves.

FLAT ROMANO BEAN SALAD WITH MINT

INSALATA DI FAGIOLINI ROMANI

I might have peppered through this book my passion for vegetables. Inspired - as always - by my family, this simple treatment can be enjoyed with any beans and is especially wonderful if they are home grown.

70 ml/5 tablespoons extra virgin olive oil
35 ml/2½ tablespoons red wine vinegar
1 garlic clove, crushed
600 g/1 lb. 5 oz. green beans (such as runner, French, flat), trimmed
2 handfuls of fresh mint, roughly chopped, plus extra to garnish
grated zest of 1 unwaxed lemon
sea salt and freshly ground black pepper

Serves 6

To make the dressing, combine the oil, vinegar and garlic with some sea salt in a small bowl. Whisk together and let stand for at least 1 hour to infuse.

Cook the beans in a saucepan of rolling, boiling, salted water until just tender. Drain, refresh in cold water and transfer to a serving bowl. Stir in the chopped mint and lemon zest, pour over the dressing and mix well. Garnish with extra mint to serve.

LEMON, FENNEL & ROCKET SALAD WITH RADICCHIO

INSALATA DI RUCOLA, FINOCCHI E LIMONE CON RADICCHIO

I am particularly fond of this salad. Please don't be put off by the lemons, they really make it very delicious. Lemons grow profusely in the south of Italy and they are sweet enough to eat. Not only are they good for you, they're enormously versatile - I think a lemon will improve the flavour of any dish. I'm also a big fan of radicchio. My father was a major importer of radicchio, which is grown in and around Verona.

½ radicchio/red chicory, torn into shreds
2 large unwaxed lemons, peeled and sliced
1 fennel head, trimmed and sliced into matchsticks
generous handful of rocket/arugula, torn into shreds
2 tablespoons good-quality extra virgin olive oil
2 tablespoons freshly grated Parmesan cheese
a few drops of balsamic vinegar
sea salt and freshly ground black pepper

Serves 4

Arrange the radicchio on 4 individual plates. Add the lemon slices, fennel and torn rocket.

To make the dressing, mix together the olive oil, Parmesan, vinegar and salt and pepper in a small bowl or jug. Pour the dressing over the salad just before serving.

SUMMER VEGETABLE STEW

CIAMBOTTA

Also known as *cianfotto*, this is a wonderful summer vegetable stew. It has many names, but this is my Nonna Ferrigno's recipe, which I treasure. Serve with good bread for mopping up all the juice. Please feel free to interchange the vegetables as you prefer. It really is a celebration of summer and what might be growing in your garden.

2 small aubergines/eggplant, cut into 2-cm/³⁄₄-in. cubes
3–4 tablespoons olive oil
1 red onion, chopped
2 teaspoons fennel seeds, crushed
2 fat garlic cloves, crushed
2 new potatoes (preferably Italian), peeled and cut into 2-cm/³⁄₄-in. cubes
1 courgette/zucchini, cut into 2-cm/³⁄₄-in. cubes
2 red (bell) peppers, cut into 2-cm/³⁄₄-in. cubes
400 g/14 oz. good-quality can of plum tomatoes or (in the summer, when ripe) 400 g/14 oz. fresh tomatoes, deseeded and chopped
sea salt and freshly ground black pepper
2 tablespoons extra virgin olive oil, for anointing
handful of fresh flat-leaf parsley, roughly chopped, to serve

Serves 6 generously

Sprinkle the aubergine with salt, place in a colander, cover with a plate and weigh down. Leave for 15 minutes.

Heat the olive oil in a medium-sized saucepan or casserole dish. Add the onion and fry for 5–10 minutes until coloured, then add the fennel seeds and allow the aromatics to be released.

Rinse the aubergine cubes and pat dry with paper towels. Add to the pan and coat and colour in the oil. Once the aubergine has coloured, add all the remaining ingredients. Simmer gently for 25–30 minutes until the vegetables are tender.

Season to taste with salt and pepper and serve hot with a sprinkling of parsley and good extra virgin olive oil.

CAULIFLOWER FROM AMALFI
CAVALFIORE DI AMALFI

This is a wonderful way of preparing cauliflower. You will never enjoy cauliflower cheese in quite the same way again. My husband repeatedly says that it is the best treatment for cauliflower ever. My tip is to cook the cauliflower with some freshly torn bay leaves to add a subtle exotic flavour, and also to eliminate the smell of cauliflower. All the brassica family benefit from this treatment. Cauliflower in Italy is usually enjoyed in the winter months.

1 cauliflower, broken into florets
3 fresh bay leaves, broken into pieces
2 large/US extra-large eggs
4 tablespoons freshly grated Parmesan cheese, plus shavings to garnish
2–3 tablespoons Italian '00' flour
3–4 tablespoons olive oil, for frying (quantity depends on the size of your cauliflower)
sea salt and freshly ground black pepper
fresh flat-leaf parsley, to garnish

Serves 6

Plunge the cauliflower into a pan of rolling boiling water, add the bay leaves and cook for 6 minutes. Immediately drain the cauliflower and plunge into iced water. Drain and pat dry, discarding the pieces of bay leaves.

Beat the eggs with the cheese and seasoning (I like plenty of salt and pepper, so will leave this for you to gauge) in a shallow bowl. Place the flour in another shallow bowl. When the cauliflower is cold and dry, coat first in the flour, one floret at a time, then dip the florets in the egg and cheese mixture.

Heat the oil in a solid, medium-sized frying pan/skillet. When hot, add the florets one at a time. Fry until golden brown on all sides and transfer to a serving plate. Sprinkle over the parsley and Parmesan shavings to garnish.

SALAD WITH AUBERGINE & ONIONS
INSALATA DI MELANZANE E CIPOLLE

This is a glorious salad, filled with the happiest of memories from my Nonna's kitchen, packed with the most wonderful flavours, all relying heavily on sun-drenched ingredients at their very best.

1 firm, glossy aubergine/eggplant
200 g/7 oz. new potatoes, peeled and sliced
2 red onions, finely chopped
handful of fresh mint, chopped
handful of fresh oregano, chopped
1½–2 tablespoons white wine vinegar
3 tablespoons good-quality extra virgin olive oil
1 chopped sun-ripened tomato, to garnish
sea salt and freshly ground black pepper
fresh bread, to serve

Serves 6

Peel and boil the whole aubergine for at least 15 minutes in plenty of boiling water until tender when pierced with the tip of a knife. Drain and cool. Cut into strips and place on a serving plate.

Boil the potatoes in a saucepan of boiling water until tender when pierced with the tip of a knife. Drain and add to the aubergine.

Add the onion to the aubergine and potato, as well as the herbs, vinegar and oil. Season with salt and pepper and mix well. Serve at room temperature and, as with most salads, accompany with some good bread to mop up all the delicious juices.

AUBERGINE & PARMESAN BAKE

PARMIGIANA DI MELANZANA

One of my all-time favourite recipes, my father used to ask me to make this whenever he was coming to stay. I feel particularly proud of this recipe; it is different from most and it is firmly rooted as my family's heritage. It is a labour of love to make, but worth the extra effort. There is quite a bit of frying, so throw open your doors and windows, get some dramatic music on and enjoy the whole process.

2 firm and glossy aubergines/
    eggplant, thinly sliced
    (see Note below)
100 ml/generous ⅓ cup olive oil
1 onion, sliced
900 g/2 lb. fresh, ripe
    tomatoes, deseeded and
    chopped
2 garlic cloves, crushed
very generous handful of fresh
    basil leaves, torn
2 tablespoons Italian '00' flour
4-5 large/US extra-large eggs
6 tablespoons freshly grated
    Parmesan
350 g/12 oz. mozzarella
    cheese, sliced
sea salt and freshly ground
    black pepper

23-cm/9-in. springform cake pan
    or 20 x 20-cm/8 x 8-in. deep
    square baking dish

Serves 6

Sprinkle the aubergine with salt, place in a colander, cover with a plate and weigh down. Leave for 25-30 minutes.

In a medium sized saucepan, heat 2 tablespoons of the olive oil, add the onion and cook gently until softened. Add the tomatoes, garlic and seasoning and simmer for 30 minutes. I usually add a few of the basil leaves at this point too, to add more flavour to the sauce. Please keep an eye on the liquid content of the sauce as it needs to be fairly concentrated. Adjust the seasoning as needed - this sauce very much depends on the quality of the tomatoes so will need tasting to check.

Rinse the aubergine slices and pat dry on paper towels. Place the flour in a shallow bowl. Whisk the eggs in another shallow bowl, season with salt and pepper and add the Parmesan (reserving a little for a garnish). Dip the aubergine slices in the flour.

Heat the remaining oil in a large frying pan/skillet over a medium heat. Dip the aubergines, one at a time, in the egg mixture and fry for 2-3 minutes on each side until golden and like soft pillows. Drain the slices on paper towels and set aside.

Preheat the oven to 180°C fan/200°C/400°F/gas 6.

Assemble the dish in the springform pan or baking dish. Place a layer of aubergines on the bottom and top with one third of the sauce, mozzarella and basil. Add the remaining layers in the same order, pressing firmly after the completion of each layer, finishing with a layer of aubergine slices. Sprinkle over the reserved Parmesan to finish. Bake in the preheated oven for 20-25 minutes until golden.

NOTE: *It is important that the aubergine is sliced as thinly as possible as it needs to be able to cook quickly.*

BROAD BEAN SALAD

INSALATA DI FAVE

This is a splendid recipe that never needs altering, and I always wait with eager anticipation for the broad/fava beans to be ripe and ready from my garden to enjoy this recipe at its best. I've even been served broad beans in their shells on a dish of ice; the importance of super fresh has a whole new meaning. They are also often enjoyed very young out of the pods with a glass of wine. This recipe comes from the world-renowned Convento di Amalfi dei Cappliccini restaurant.

1 fennel bulb
zest and juice of 1 lemon
1.5 kg/3¾ lb. fresh young broad/fava
    beans, shelled
2 red onions, very thinly sliced into rings
generous handful of fresh mint leaves,
    torn
250 g/9 oz. soft, barely salted sheep or
    goats' cheese
3 tablespoons superb extra virgin olive oil
sea salt and freshly ground black pepper

Serves 6

Shave the fennel very finely on a mandolin. Add a few drops of lemon juice to a bowl of water and drop in the shaved fennel.

Place the broad beans in a pan of boiling water and cook for 7 minutes, depending on the size. When they are tender, immediately drop them into a bowl of iced water. This will help them keep their texture and colour. Pod the beans again to reveal their beautiful vibrant green.

Drain the fennel. Arrange the beans on a plate along with the fennel, onion rings, mint and cheese. Mix the extra virgin olive oil with the juice of the lemon and add the zest, salt and pepper to make a dressing. When ready to eat, dress this amazingly tasty, historic salad.

ROCKET & FIG SALAD

INSALATA DI RUCOLA E FICHI

Rocket/arugula is a member of the same family as mustard and cress, which is obvious when you bite into it and encounter its bitter, sharp and peppery flavour. It was once cultivated in Britain but went out of fashion for centuries until recently, when Italian imports (such as my father) caused a happy renaissance. There are many different varieties of rocket; I love the selvatica wild variety for instance. Super ripe figs make a big difference to this salad.

225 g/8 oz. rocket/arugula leaves
200 g/7 oz. fresh, ripe figs, quartered
1 tablespoon freshly squeezed lemon juice
zest of 1 unwaxed lemon
2–3 tablespoons extra virgin olive oil
handful of Parmesan shavings (optional)
sea salt and freshly ground black pepper

Serves 6

Wash the rocket well and dry it thoroughly. Mix the quartered figs with the rocket in a serving bowl.

Mix the lemon juice, zest, oil, salt and pepper together well in a small bowl or jug and pour over the leaves and figs. Arrange the Parmesan shavings on top, if using.

SWEET & SOUR COURGETTES
ZUCCHINI SCAPECE

Contorni at their very best. I just simply adore this treatment that is also adopted for anchovies and fish. By all accounts, it is as a result of the Spanish occupation of the area. If we continue to have hot summers, it is possible to dry courgettes/zucchini on a sunny terrace, and I have been successful many times. You can even place a tray of courgettes to dry on the roof of your car on a hot day. This is a spectacularly simple dish, but do follow the recipe closely to guarantee success. You will want to make double batches.

9 courgettes/zucchini, cut into thin slices lengthways (see Note below)
175 ml/¾ cup olive oil
generous handful of fresh mint
3 garlic cloves, crushed
4 tablespoons white wine vinegar
4–6 tablespoons good-quality extra virgin olive oil
sea salt and freshly ground black pepper
fresh bread, to serve

Serves 6

Place all the courgette strips on a wooden board and leave in a very sunny spot for at least 3 hours, turning them over periodically – this is my Nonna's traditional method. Alternatively, put them on a parchment-lined baking sheet in a low oven preheated to 120°C fan/140°C/275°F/gas 1 for 1½ hours to dry out, turning occasionally – this method concentrates the flavour and is well worth the effort.

Heat the olive oil in a large frying pan/skillet and fry the dried courgette strips for about 2 minutes in batches until golden. Drain on paper towels.

When cold, transfer the fried courgettes to a serving dish, sprinkle with salt and pepper to taste, then add the mint, garlic, vinegar and extra virgin olive oil. Cover and leave to marinate for 3 hours. Serve with good bread to mop up the juices.

NOTES:
• *Choose skinny courgettes where you can as they will have more flavour and be less bitter than larger ones.*

• *If you are brave enough to use a mandolin when slicing the courgettes, this will save time. The slices must be thin, but not too thin – you want to have some texture.*

FRIED FENNEL

COTOLETTE DI FINOCCHI

In Piedmont, vegetables such as fennel, artichokes, celery and the white stalks of Swiss chard
are often coated in egg and breadcrumbs and fried in butter. I like fennel best.

6 Florence fennel bulbs (3 male,
   3 female), cleaned, trimmed and
   cut into wedges
2 large/US extra-large eggs
225 g/2¾ cups dried fine breadcrumbs
40 g/3 tablespoons unsalted butter
45 ml/3 tablespoons olive oil
freshly grated Parmesan (optional)
sea salt and freshly ground black pepper

Serves 6

Cook the fennel in a saucepan of boiling water for 10 minutes. Drain
and pat dry with paper towels.

Beat the eggs with a pinch of salt and pepper in a shallow bowl. Tip the
breadcrumbs into another shallow bowl.

Dip the fennel wedges in the egg, then coat with breadcrumbs, patting
so that the crumbs adhere firmly to each piece.

Melt the butter and oil in a large frying pan/skillet and fry the fennel
until the crumbs are golden brown on all sides. Drain on paper towels
and serve with a sprinkling of grated Parmesan cheese, if desired.

ROASTED PEACHES, BURRATA, BASIL & LEMON
WITH COURGETTE SHAVINGS

PESCHE GRIGLIATI CON BURRATA E BASILICO

Roasting the peaches intensifies their natural sweetness. This is a wonderful way to enjoy this delicious fruit
in a different manner, rather than just eating them fresh.

3 sun-ripened peaches, cut in half
   and stoned/pitted
1 thin courgette/zucchini, grated
1 ball of burrata
handful of fresh basil, leaves torn
grated zest of 1 unwaxed lemon
good-quality extra virgin olive oil,
   for drizzling
sea salt and freshly ground black pepper

Serves 6

Preheat the grill/broiler to medium.

Season the peaches with salt and pepper. Arrange the grated courgette
over the peaches and grill/broil for about 4 minutes until golden.

While still warm, place the peaches and courgette in a serving bowl and
add the burrata in dollops. Garnish with fresh basil, lemon zest and a
touch of extra virgin olive oil to serve.

PRESERVED TOMATOES WITH OREGANO
POMODORI SECCHI CON ORIGANO

Tomatoes can become a problem on the Amalfi coast; our beautiful scarlet sun-ripened tomatoes with thin skins and juicy flesh often ripen all at once. This recipe creates a rush of very happy memories of rows upon rows of tomatoes sunbathing on wooden traps on the terrace. These delicious preserved tomatoes can be made at home, so don't buy them. Lay tomatoes in the sun with salt on a beautifully hot summer's day; you will be so appreciative of this method of preserving, whether they are home grown or not. As a child, opening up *la dispensa* (the larder) and seeing rows of scarlet jars brimming with tomatoes ready to be enjoyed later in the year was utterly reassuring. They are perfect for antipasti, really delicious with bread in a panini or to add to casseroles to enrich flavours. I really hope you will have a go.

2 kg/4¼ lb. ripe, juicy plum tomatoes
generous amount of sea salt
6 garlic cloves, finely chopped or grated
4 teaspoons dried chilli/chile flakes (peperoncino)
generous handful of fresh oregano leaves
250 g/9 oz. Pecorino Romano cheese, freshly grated
good-quality extra virgin olive oil, to top

2 x 500-g/1 lb. 2-oz. jars

Makes 2 jars

Preheat the oven to 140°C fan/160°C/325°F/gas 3.

Pour water into a pan large enough to hold all the tomatoes at the same time and bring to the boil. Add the tomatoes when the water is boiling and boil for just a couple of minutes to soften the skins slightly.

Drain the tomatoes, then cut them in partially in half, taking are not to cut all the way through – they still need to be attached, like a book. Spread the tomatoes out on a baking sheet, sprinkle with salt and bake in the preheated oven for 1½ hours, or place them in the sun for at least 2 hours.

Meanwhile, prepare the seasoning by mixing together the garlic, dried chillies, oregano and grated Pecorino Romano.

Take one tomato half at a time and dip the cut side into the seasoning mixture. Put the 2 halves together, closing like a sandwich and place in the bottom of a sterilized jar, one after the other, until you reach the top. Cover with extra virgin olive oil, seal tightly and store in a cool place. You may start devouring after a week.

NOTE: *Add the dried chilli flakes to taste for this recipe – if you prefer things milder, you may not need as much as stated.*

MARINATED AUBERGINES
MELANZANE SOTT'OLIO

My grandmother used to make this in autumn when the aubergines/eggplant were ripe. I have very fond memories of what we called 'aubergine day'. We would all know that quite soon, at the end of the simple preparation, we would be enjoying aubergine sandwiches - slices of marinated vegetable squashed between two slices of country bread, oily and fragrant. This dish is best when the aubergine has had enough time to completely absorb the marinade. For this reason, start its preparation at least two days in advance.

2 aubergines/eggplant
(900 g/2 lb. in weight),
peeled and cut crosswise
into 2 cm/¾ in. thick slices
2 tablespoons white wine
vinegar
8 tablespoons good-quality
extra virgin olive oil
handful of fresh mint leaves,
chopped
2 teaspoons fresh oregano
leaves
4 garlic cloves, finely chopped
sea salt and freshly ground
black pepper

Serves 4

Dissolve 2 tablespoons salt in a large bowl of water. Add the aubergines slices and leave to soak for 30 minutes.

Combine 600 ml/2½ cups water and the vinegar in a large saucepan over a medium heat and bring to the boil. Drain the aubergine slices in a colander and add them to the water-vinegar mixture. Cook for 3 minutes at a rolling boil.

Using a slotted spoon, transfer the aubergine slices to paper towels, arranging them in a single layer. Cover with another piece of paper and press lightly to absorb the liquid. Continue, working in batches and using dry pieces of paper as you go. Drain for 1 hour.

Transfer the aubergine slices to a large bowl. Mix the oil, herbs, garlic and pepper together in a bowl or jug/pitcher and add more salt to taste if needed.

Pour this mixture over the aubergine, adding more oil if necessary to cover. Cover the bowl and leave to sit for 2 days before serving.

DESSERTS

DOLCI

DESSERTS & DRINKS

The Italian penchant for all things sweet probably originated in medieval times when the seafaring Venetians introduced cane sugar to Italy from the East. But the Arabs were also very influential; when they ruled Sicily, they brought in citrus, figs and almonds, which appear now in many Italian desserts. Perhaps the most significant Arab innovation was freezing (using snow from Mount Etna), which resulted in the *gelati* (ice creams) for which Italy is now so famous.

Most Italian meals end with a piece of fruit rather than a more elaborate dessert, and one of my most insistent childhood memories is sitting at my parents' kitchen table being fed pieces of fruit on the end of a fork by my father. He would have grown the peach or apricot himself and was testing its success on his family! Sometimes fruit is cooked – figs, peaches, apricots

and pears spring to mind – often in *Vin Santo*, a Tuscan sweet wine, or preserved to be served with ice cream. However, there are many famous and traditional Italian recipes such as *pannacotta*, *zabaglione* and, more recently, *tiramisu*. These can be bought but are occasionally made at home for a special occasion. *Delizia al limone* is a breast-shaped dessert created by a Sorrento pastry-maker in 1978; it has a base of p*an di spagna* (sponge) and is bathed in our famous lemon liqueur with lots of limoncello-flavoured cream. It is on every menu on the Amalfi Coast, and you must try it!

Tarts, pastries and cakes are very popular on the Amalfi Coast, and some say that ours are the best in the country! We often pop into the local bakery to buy a slice of tart or a pastry filled with *crema pasticceria* (custard) to take home or to a friend's house as a gift. Italians like to *passatiempo* – 'pass the time' – and are much less formal than other nationalities at knocking on a friend's door, armed with sweet delights, ready for

an hour or so of gossip! Small cakes and biscuits are eaten a lot in Italy, particularly after the siesta to give a burst of energy for the rest of the day to come. Many of these sweet things would be made with Italian soft cheeses, or chocolate, nuts or fruit – or a combination of them all! Some might include fruit preserved the year before – grapes as raisins, plums as prunes, candied citrus peel. A whole tart or cake might be bought occasionally for dessert on a special occasion. Italians love celebrating, and specific sweet things are traditionally associated with festivals such as Christmas and Easter, or with all those saints' days! For instance, *melanzane al cioccolato* (chocolate aubergine/eggplant) is a Campanian speciality for *Ferragosto*, an Italian public holiday on 15 August: slices of aubergine are layered with melted chocolate instead of tomato sauce and baked like a *parmigiana*.

Italy is famed the world over for its *gelati* (ice creams), and they originated in Sicily. By the 17th century, ice cream recipes were published and *gelaterie* opened all over the world. The famous ice-cream parlours of the USA were undoubtedly opened and run by Italian immigrants who flocked to the New World from Naples and other ports; over 5 million Italians sailed to America towards the beginning of the 20th century, fleeing the poverty-stricken regions of the south such as Campania, Calabria, Apulia and Sicily.

Most Italian *gelati* are sorbet-like, based on a sugar syrup made with fruit juice or other flavourings. The syrups are frozen, where they form crystals; these need to be small to be palatable. *Sorbetti* and *graniti* are almost crunchy because they have no fat content to soften the texture of the ice crystals. By adding fat such as milk, cream or egg yolks, the crystallization process is slowed down and inhibited, making the mixture smoother and softer. *Gelato* itself is made with cream and/or egg yolks, but is softer than the British version; this is because it has been churned more slowly, which means less air is introduced, and because it contains about half the fat.

One of my recipes is based on limoncello, the Amalfi Coast speciality liqueur. This wonderful spirit, packed with flavour, is made in turn from Amalfi lemons. These lemons are unique to the Amalfi Coast, due to the microclimate of the area – the sea salt, sunshine and occasional rain. They were developed centuries ago as a cross between small local lemons and bitter oranges, and have the most sensational juice and zest, the latter used to make limoncello. They are known as *sfusato amalfitano* in Italy and have a protected geographical status (IGP). They are cultivated in terraces all along the Amalfi Coast, supported by scaffolds of chestnut poles. Because of the narrow terracing, they all have to be picked by hand, which is back-breaking work, involving hundreds of steps up and down, the farmers bearing heavy sacks of lemons.

Once you have tried the juice or zest of an Amalfi lemon – often sold with their leaves still attached to show how fresh they are – I guarantee that you will be converted!

CAPRI CAKE

TORTA CAPRESE

This recipe originates from the beautiful island of Capri. It was originally a mistake by the chef who left out the flour and has subsequently become tremendously famous. It also boasts of being created when the King of Naples' Austrian wife requested a Sacher; Neapolitan chefs improvised and this cake was the result. As with everything, please use the freshest of ingredients. This cake is always extremely well received on my cooking classes. I truly hope you will enjoy it, too.

200 g/generous ¾ cup unsalted butter, plus extra for greasing

250 g/1¼ cups golden caster/superfine sugar

5 large/US extra-large eggs, separated

250 g/9 oz. dark chocolate, 70% cocoa solids, melted

250 g/9 oz. almonds, toasted until golden brown and finely chopped

grated zest of 1 large unwaxed lemon

sifted icing/powdered sugar, for dusting

23-cm/9-in. round cake tin

Serves 8

Preheat the oven to 180°C fan/200°C/400°F/gas 6. Grease and line the cake tin with baking paper.

Place the butter in a heatproof bowl set over a saucepan of simmering water. Add the sugar and mix to a creamy consistency. Add the egg yolks, mix together, then add the melted chocolate and almonds.

Whisk the egg whites in a separate bowl until they form soft peaks. Add the grated lemon zest and egg whites to the chocolate mixture and carefully fold in a clockwise direction until completely combined.

Turn the mixture into the prepared cake tin and bake in the preheated oven for 30 minutes. The cake will still have a little wobble when it comes out of the oven.

Cool on a wire rack and dust with icing sugar when cold.

NOTE: *I like to serve this cake with either lemon or almond gelato, or just mascarpone, to which a little vanilla and lemon juice have been added.*

AMALFI LEMON TART

TORTA DI LIMONE DI AMALFI

This is the ultimate lemon cake with the best texture and crumb. You will make it time and time again and never tire of this wonderful recipe from my Nonno. I am so grateful that I have this recipe. When soaked with rum and served with fruit and cream, it is perfect for celebrations.

zest and juice of 3 unwaxed lemons
5 large/US extra-large eggs
350 g/1¾ cups caster/ superfine sugar
pinch of sea salt
540 ml/2¼ cups double/ heavy cream
275 g/2 cups Italian '00' flour, plus extra for dusting
1 tablespoon baking powder
100 g/3½ oz. melted unsalted butter, plus extra for greasing
3 teaspoons vanilla extract
1 tablespoon apricot jam
200 g/1½ cups icing/powdered sugar

26-cm/10¼-in. non-stick baking tin

Serves 6-8

Preheat the oven to 160°C fan/180°C/350°F/gas 4. Grease and line the baking tin with baking paper.

Place the lemon zest, eggs, sugar and salt in the bowl of a stand mixer and beat at a high speed for at least 10 minutes until the mixture is light and mousse-like. Fold in the cream.

Sieve the flour and baking powder together, then fold that into the wet mixture. Lastly, gently fold in the cooled melted butter and vanilla. Spoon into the cake tin and bake in the preheated oven for about 55 minutes.

Turn the cake out onto a wire rack to cool but leave the oven on. When the cake is cold, brush with apricot jam all over the surface and sides.

Make a glaze. Put the juice of 2 of the lemons and the icing sugar in a saucepan over a medium heat until the sugar melts and is syrupy. Brush the syrup all over the cake and sides and return the cake to the oven (just placed on the oven rack) for 1 minute to set the jam and syrup. This will also improve the keeping quality of the cake.

PEAR, HAZELNUT & RICOTTA CAKE
TORTA DI RICOTTA E PERE

This cake was made famous by Sal De Riso, the fantastic patisserie in Minori. In their version the pears are cooked in rum. I've served this often at dinner parties and it is very impressive. The cake layers are meant to be thin, so don't be alarmed.

SPONGE

100 g/3¹/₂ oz. hazelnuts
50 g/¹/₃ cup Italian '00' flour
100 g/¹/₂ cup caster/superfine sugar
75 g/¹/₃ cup unsalted butter, cut into 4 pieces, plus extra for greasing
4 large/US extra-large egg whites
icing/powdered sugar, for dusting

FILLING

2-3 pears, peeled, cored and cut into bite-sized pieces
1 vanilla pod/bean, split lengthways in half, or 1 teaspoon vanilla extract
125 g/²/₃ cup golden caster/ superfine sugar
250 g/9 oz. ricotta, drained
100 g/3¹/₂ oz. double/heavy cream

2 x 20-cm/8-in. round cake tins

Serves 6-8

Preheat the oven to 160°C fan/180°C/350°F/gas 4. Grease the cake tins with butter and line the bottoms with baking paper.

Scatter the hazelnuts on a baking sheet and toast in the oven for 10 minutes. Remove from the oven and leave to cool but leave the oven on.

Use a food processor to blitz the roasted nuts. Add the flour, sugar and butter to the food processor and whizz again to blend.

In a large bowl, whisk the egg whites to soft peaks, then fold them into the nut mixture. Pour into the prepared tins and bake in the preheated oven for 20 minutes. Remove from the oven and leave to cool for 5 minutes before turning out onto wire racks. Peel off the circles of baking paper.

To make the filling, put the pears, vanilla, 75 g/¹/₃ cup of the sugar and 75 ml/¹/₃ cup water in a saucepan. Cook for 15-20 minutes, depending on the ripeness of the pears, until they are soft. This is best done with a circle of baking paper pressed down on top of the pears to trap in the steam. When the pears are soft, strain them through a sieve resting over a bowl to collect the juices and set aside.

Whisk together the remaining sugar with the ricotta and cream in a bowl until smooth and thick. When the pears are cool, stir them into the cream. Place one hazelnut sponge on a board and spoon the filling over. Lay the other sponge on top and push down so that the filling oozes out a little. Smooth the sides with the back of a spoon. Sift the icing sugar over the top and transfer to a serving dish or cake stand. Serve in slices with the syrup from the pears for drizzling.

TIP: *I often drizzle chocolate over the top of the sponge in a squiggle and sprinkle over extra hazelnuts - this gives a very contemporary look.*

MY GRANDMOTHER'S ITALIAN GATEAU
TORTA DELLA MIA NONNA

I have published this recipe before, but I can't resist including it again, as I have wonderful memories of it being served at special family gatherings, birthdays and feast days. It can be served as an Italian wedding cake, and it is the sort of thing that the local trattoria would do for such an occasion, calling it *'torta della casa'*. Make it for your family celebrations.

6 large/US extra-large eggs
175 g/generous ¾ cup caster/
    superfine sugar
175 g/1⅓ cups plain/all-purpose
    or Italian '00' flour, plus extra
    for dusting

CONFECTIONERS' CUSTARD
2 tablespoons plain/all-purpose
    or Italian '00' flour
2 tablespoons caster/superfine
    sugar
1 large/US extra-large egg
finely grated zest of 1 unwaxed
    lemon (optional)
½ teaspoon vanilla extract
300 ml/1¼ cups whole milk

BUTTER CREAM
175 g/¾ cup unsalted butter,
    plus extra for greasing
175 g/1¼ cups icing/powdered
    sugar, plus 1 tablespoon
1 large/US extra-large egg
100 ml/generous ⅓ cup cold
    strong black coffee

TOPPING
3 tablespoons dark rum
300 ml/1¼ cups double/heavy
    cream
a few drops of vanilla extract
5 tablespoons toasted flaked
    almonds or hazelnuts, or
    a mixture of both
seasonal fruit or flowers
    to decorate (optional)

deep 30-cm/12-in. or 23-cm/9-in.
    round cake tin

Serves 10–12

To make the cake, put the eggs and sugar in a heatproof bowl and set it over a saucepan of gently simmering water. Use an electric whisk to whisk until thick and creamy. Gently sift in the flour, a little at a time, and fold in. Pour into the prepared tin. Bake in the preheated oven – 18–20 minutes if baking in the larger tin or 35–40 minutes for the smaller tin – until risen and golden. Turn out and leave to cool on a wire rack.

To make the custard, mix the flour, sugar, egg, lemon zest, if using, and vanilla extract together in a bowl. Gently heat the milk in a saucepan but do not allow it to boil. Gradually pour the hot milk into the egg and flour mixture. Return the mixture to the saucepan and heat very gently, stirring constantly with a wooden spoon, until the mixture thickens. Remove from the heat and place a piece of baking paper over the custard to prevent a skin forming. Leave to cool.

To make the butter cream, beat the butter and the 175 g/1¼ cups icing sugar together in a bowl. In a separate bowl, beat the egg with the remaining tablespoon of sugar. Add the egg and sugar mixture to the butter mixture. Use an electric whisk to very gently add the coffee (as it can split) and mix until thick and creamy.

To assemble the cake, cut it horizontally into 3 even layers. Spoon the custard on one layer and spread the butter cream on the second, then sandwich the slices together. Gently pour the rum over the top to soak into the cake.

Whip the cream and vanilla extract in a large bowl until it just holds its shape, then use it to cover the top and sides of the cake. Gently press the nuts onto the sides of the cake and decorate with fresh fruit or flowers as desired. Chill before serving.

STUFFED FIGS
FICHI FARCITI

The memory of picking figs straight from the trees as a child in Italy gives these fruits a sort of magic quality for me. I used to run home with armfuls of them, passing hundreds more squashed in the road. There are so many wonderful ways to eat figs, but of all the recipes, this is my favourite.

12 ripe fresh figs
55 g/2 oz. walnut halves, freshly shelled if possible, roughly chopped
3 tablespoons fragrant honey
3 tablespoons vermouth
115 g/4 oz. mascarpone
115 g/4 oz. dark chocolate, 75% cocoa solids, broken into chunks

Serves 6

Preheat the oven to 180°C fan/200°C/400°F/gas 6.

Cut a tiny slice off the bottom of each fig so that it will sit upright.

Make 2 crossways cuts down through the top of the figs, about 2.5 cm/1 in. deep, and ease the figs open.

Mix the walnuts, honey, vermouth and mascarpone together in a bowl, then spoon the mixture into the opened-out fig cavity. Bake in the preheated oven for 10–15 minutes.

Meanwhile, melt the chocolate in a heatproof bowl set over a pan of simmering water.

Place 2 figs on each plate and drizzle with the melted chocolate to serve.

STUFFED APRICOTS

ALBICOCCHE RIPIENE

In the early summer, the orchard at the Hotel Santa Caterina provides the chef Eolo with fresh apricots, which he stuffs with amaretti biscuits and poaches in amaretti liqueur. This recipe reminds me of Mummy who was a passionate apricot lover. Apricots that are fully ripe yet firm are perfect for this dish. The best amaretti biscuits come in a red box marked *'di Saronna'*.

10 large, firm apricots (about 1.25 kg/2¾ lb. in total), peeled, cut in half and stoned/pitted
25 g/1 oz. unsalted butter
3 tablespoons caster/superfine sugar
165 ml/⅔ cup amaretti liqueur
12 amaretti biscuits, crushed
pine nuts, to decorate (optional)

Serves 4

Cut 2 of the apricot halves into large chunks and set aside. Slightly enlarge the hollows of the remaining halves using a melon baller.

Melt the butter in a large non-stick frying pan/skillet. Add the sugar and cook over a medium heat, stirring constantly, until the sugar dissolves and is a light caramel colour. Pour in the liqueur and simmer, stirring, for 2 minutes – it will splutter, so wear oven gloves.

Add half the apricots to this syrup and poach for 5–10 minutes until almost tender (test by piercing with a small sharp knife). Remove with a slotted spoon and drain, inverted, on a shallow plate. Cook the remaining apricots in the same way.

Add the crumbled biscuits to the syrup left in the pan. Cook over a low heat, crushing the crumbs with the back of a wooden spoon until they have melted into a coarse purée. Scrape the contents of the pan into a food processor or blender, add the reserved apricot chunks and process until smooth. Return the mixture to the pan and simmer slowly until brown in colour. Leave to cool in the pan for 5 minutes. Spoon equal amounts of the filling into the hollows of the apricots. Decorate the top of each apricot with pine nuts, if using.

CHOCOLATE BISCOTTI WITH PISTACHIOS
BISCOTTI MORBIDI CON CIOCCOLATO

High up in the Minori mountainside we celebrate many varieties of nuts. This recipe marries together
two of my lifelong passions - and coupled with espresso, it is heavenly!

250 g/generous 1³/₄ cups Italian '00' flour,
  plus extra for dusting
65 g/2¹/₂ oz. Dutch-processed quality
  cocoa powder
5 ml/1 teaspoon baking powder
pinch of sea salt
100 g/3¹/₂ oz. good-quality chocolate chunks,
  70-75% cocoa solids, roughly chopped
150 g/5¹/₄ oz. pistachios
100 g/3¹/₂ oz. butter, softened,
  plus extra for greasing
225 g/generous 1 cup caster/superfine sugar
2 large/US extra-large eggs

Makes 16

Preheat the oven to 180°C fan/200°C/400°F/gas 6.

Grease a baking sheet with a little butter and dust lightly with flour.

Combine the flour, cocoa, baking powder, salt, chocolate and pistachios
in a bowl.

In another bowl, beat together the butter and sugar until pale and fluffy.
Add the eggs and beat until well combined.

Stir in the flour mixture until it forms a stiff dough. Place the dough onto
the baking sheet and press into a 30 x 10 cm/12 x 4 in. rectangle shape.
Bake in the preheated oven for 35 minutes. Remove from the oven and
leave to cool on a wire rack to room temperature.

Slice into thick fingers and serve with coffee or gelato.

FIG, APRICOT & PISTACHIO BISCOTTI
BISCOTTI DI FICO, ALBICOCCA E PISTACCHIO

Biscotti are famous the world over, arranged neatly on trays in coffee shops. Cantuccini are smaller versions. Please
try out as many different flavour combinations as you can muster. This is a firm favourite of friends and family alike.

200 g/1¹/₂ cups Italian '00' flour,
  plus extra for dusting
pinch of sea salt
1¹/₂ teaspoons baking powder
100 g/¹/₂ cup caster/superfine sugar
grated zest of 1 orange
60 g/2 oz. shelled pistachio nuts
30 g/1 oz. raisins
40 g/1¹/₂ oz. dried apricots
40 g/1¹/₂ oz. dried figs
1 teaspoon vanilla extract
2 large/US extra-large eggs

Makes 18

Preheat the oven to 150°C fan/170°C/325°F/gas 3. Line 2 baking
sheets with baking paper.

Mix the flour, salt and baking powder in a large bowl. Add the sugar,
orange zest, nuts, dried fruits and vanilla extract.

Mix the eggs together in a small bowl with a fork and add to the dry
ingredients. Bring the dough together with the fork until you get a ball
that is relatively smooth (not cracked). Flour the work surface and roll
the dough into a log. Flatten it slightly so that it is about 8 cm/3 in. wide
and place on one of the baking sheets. Bake in the preheated oven for
about 30 minutes. Remove from the oven and leave to cool.

Use a serrated knife to slice the log into 5 mm/¹/₈ in. slices and lay them
on the lined baking sheets. Bake in the oven to crisp up for 8-10 minutes,
turning them halfway through the cooking time. Leave to cool on a wire
rack. Enjoy with gelato and coffee.

LITTLE JAM PASTRIES

BOCCONOTTI

A true Amalfi experience with simply hundreds and hundreds of variations. This happens to be my favourite. These are excellent with a strong espresso.

1 large/US extra-large egg
15 g/1 tablespoon caster/
   superfine sugar
15 g/1 tablespoon Italian '00'
   flour
100 ml/generous $\frac{1}{3}$ cup single/
   light cream
zest of $\frac{1}{2}$ unwaxed lemon
a few drops of vanilla extract
30 ml/2 tablespoons cherry
   jam
1 egg yolk, beaten

PASTA FROLLA
250 g/generous $1\frac{3}{4}$ cup Italian
   '00' flour
75 g/$\frac{1}{2}$ cup icing/powdered
   sugar, plus extra for dusting
125 g/$4\frac{1}{2}$ oz. unsalted butter
1 large/US extra-large egg
pinch of sea salt
a few drops vanilla extract
grated zest of 1 unwaxed lemon

Makes 24

To make a pastry cream, cream together the egg and sugar until pale and thick. Sift in the flour and beat until smooth. Heat the cream and lemon zest in a saucepan until almost boiling, then pour onto the egg mixture, stirring all the time. Return to the pan and cook over a low heat until it thickens. Remove the pan from the heat and stir in the vanilla. Cover the surface with baking paper and leave to cool completely.

Preheat the oven to 200°C fan/220°C/425°F/gas 7.

For the *pasta frolla*, mix all the ingredients together in the bowl of a food processor or blender. Pulse to bring all the ingredients together to form a damp but not wet dough. Remove from the bowl, wrap in baking paper and chill in the fridge for at least 30 minutes.

Place the pastry on a floured surface, roll it out and cut into 7 cm/2 in. circles. Place just a tiny dab of jam and pastry cream in the centre of each circle. Fold the circle in half and press the edges firmly together to seal well. Lay the pastries on a baking tray and brush with the egg yolk.

Bake in the preheated oven for 15 minutes until golden brown. Leave to cool, then dust with icing sugar.

BAKED SWEET PASTRIES
MINNI DI SANTA AGATHA

These dome-shaped pastries are made from a sweet pasta dough. Their shape has inspired the name which, literally translated, means 'breasts of Saint Agatha'. During a recent teaching trip in Italy, representatives of a major supermarket chain, who were attending, became very excited by this recipe, feeling it could be marketed as an Italian version of a Christmas mince pie. It certainly has as much diversity in its flavour and, in fact, tastes divine!

PASTRY

225 g/1¾ cups plain/
    all-purpose or Italian '00'
    flour, plus extra for dusting
65 g/⅓ cup caster/superfine
    sugar
100 g/3½ oz. unsalted butter,
    cut into pieces, plus extra
    for greasing
1 large/US extra-large egg
1 tablespoon finely grated
    unwaxed lemon zest
pinch of sea salt
icing/powdered sugar and
    cocoa powder, for dusting

FILLING

225 g/8 oz. ricotta cheese
55 g/¼ cup caster/superfine
    sugar
1½ teaspoons vanilla extract
1 large/US extra-large egg yolk
1 tablespoon candied orange
    peel or mixed peel, finely
    chopped
1 tablespoon shelled hazelnuts,
    toasted and finely chopped
25 g/1 oz. plain chocolate,
    50% cocoa solids, grated

Makes about 12

To make the pastry, put the flour and sugar in a food processor and, working on full speed, add the butter pieces gradually until well mixed. With the food processor still running, add the egg, lemon zest and salt. Turn the dough out onto baking paper, flatten, cover and chill in the fridge for 30 minutes. Allow to come back to room temperature before rolling.

Push the ricotta through a sieve into a bowl. Stir in the sugar, vanilla extract, egg yolk, peel, hazelnuts and chocolate until well mixed.

Preheat the oven to 160°C fan/180°C/350°F/gas 4. Grease a large baking sheet.

Roll out the pastry on a floured surface until about 5 mm/⅛ in. thick (see Note below). Use a 7-cm/3-in. cutter to cut out about 24 circles. Put 2 teaspoons of filling on half the pastry circles and top each with another pastry circle. Press the edges to seal all round.

Place the pastries on the greased baking sheet and prick the top of each one with the tines of a fork. Bake in the preheated oven for 20 minutes until golden. Leave to cool, then dredge with icing sugar and cocoa powder.

NOTE: *You will need very light hands when rolling out this pastry. If you are finding it troublesome, you could roll it between layers of cling film/plastic wrap instead.*

RUM BABA

BABA NAPOLETANO

This recipe is dedicated to my grandpa and father, who both relished this dessert and considered this the ultimate treat. This dessert is typical of the region and there are, as happens frequently, many, many variations. They can be bought, even in jars, but freshly made is incomparable. If you can't find the moulds, muffin cases will work, but adjust the baking time. They can also be brushed with apricot jam.

BABA MIXTURE
50 ml/3½ tablespoons whole milk
50 g/3½ tablespoons unsalted butter, for greasing
25 g/1 oz. fresh yeast or 14 g/ ½ oz. dried active yeast
2 large/US extra-large egg yolks and 1 egg
50 g/3½ tablespoons caster/ superfine sugar
1 teaspoon vanilla extract
zest of 1 unwaxed lemon
50 g/1¾ oz. raisins
225 g/1¾ cups strong white flour, plus extra for dusting

RUM SAUCE
125 g/scant ⅔ cup caster/ superfine sugar
2 lemon slices
1 orange slice
1 cinnamon stick
50 ml/3½ tablespoons dark rum

Individual baba moulds:
6 cm/2¼ in. in height, 4 cm/ 1½ in. in diameter at the base, 5 cm/2 in. diameter at the top

Makes 8–10 baba

Grease and flour the moulds.

Gently heat the milk and butter until the butter has melted. Remove from the heat and leave to cool until hand hot. Cream the yeast together with 2 tablespoons of the warm milk mixture.

Mix the egg yolks and sugar together in a large bowl until thick and creamy, then add the egg, vanilla, lemon zest, raisins, flour and the yeast mixture. Mix well with a wooden spoon until it forms a dough. Place the dough in an oiled bowl and cover with a damp clean tea towel. Leave to rise in a warm place for 2 hours until doubled in size.

Preheat the oven to 160°C fan/180°C/350°F/gas 4.

Turn the dough out onto a lightly floured surface and knead lightly until smooth. Place 70 g/2¾ oz. balls of dough into each mould and leave to rise again until the dough grows into the mould and forms a dome on top.

Bake in the preheated oven for 25 minutes, then leave to cool in the moulds for 15 minutes.

Meanwhile, make the rum sauce by heating all of the ingredients together in a saucepan over medium heat for about 7 minutes.

Serve the babas with the rum sauce.

NECTARINE & ALMOND TART
TORTA DI PESCHE, NETTARINE E MANDORLE

A heavenly combination of flavours. Please experiment with other fruits in season - figs work well, as do raspberries and plums. This recipe relies on my mother's perfect, obedient and fail-safe Italian pastry: *Pasta Frolla.*

PASTA FROLLA
250 g/generous 1¾ cups
    Italian '00' flour, plus extra
    for dusting
75 g/½ cup icing/powdered
    sugar
125 g/generous ½ cup unsalted
    butter
1 large/US extra-large egg
pinch of sea salt
few drops of vanilla extract
grated zest of 1 unwaxed lemon

FILLING
150 g/⅔ cup unsalted butter,
    softened
150 g/¾ cup golden caster/
    superfine sugar
3 large/US extra-large eggs
75 g/2¾ oz. ground almonds
grated zest of 1 unwaxed lemon
75 g/generous ½ cup Italian
    '00' flour
¼ teapoon baking powder
1 teaspoon vanilla extract
400 g/14 oz. nectarine slices
    (without stones/pits),
    ripe is best (about 6-8
    nectarines, depending
    on size)
2 tablespoons flaked almonds
2 tablespoons apricot
    conserve

deep 23-cm/9-in. loose-bottomed
    tart tin

Serves 6-8

For the *pasta frolla*, mix all the ingredients together in the bowl of a food processor. Pulse to bring everything together to form a damp but not wet dough. Remove from the bowl, wrap in baking paper and chill in the fridge for at least 30 minutes.

Meanwhile, make the filling. Mix the butter, sugar, eggs, ground almonds, lemon zest, flour, baking powder and vanilla together until well combined.

Preheat the oven to 180°C fan/200°C/400°F/gas 6.

Roll out 250 g/9 oz. of the pastry on a floured surface and use it to line the tart tin. The remaining pastry can be frozen for up to 1 month or wrapped and chilled and used the next day.

Chill the lined tart tin the fridge for 10 minutes; this prevents shrinkage of the pastry.

After the pastry has been chilled, spoon the filling into the tart tin. Arrange the nectarine slices on top of mixture and scatter the flaked almonds over the top. Bake for 40-45 minutes until the tart has risen and is golden brown.

Melt the apricot conserve with 1 tablespoon water in a small saucepan. Brush the melted conserve over the top of the tart as a glaze and leave to cool. Cut into slices and serve.

NEAPOLITAN RICOTTA TART

PASTIERA NAPOLETANA

I thought I ought to have one sweet pasta dish in this book. There are many variations of this famous and rich classical dish from the Cappuccini Convent in Amalfi. I think it's best eaten the day after it is made.

PASTRY

125 g/generous ½ cup
   unsalted butter
75 g/generous ½ cup icing/
   powdered sugar
1 large/US extra-large egg
250 g/1¾ cups Italian '00'
   flour, plus more for dusting

FILLING

450 g/1 lb. ricotta cheese
115 g/generous ½ cup caster/
   superfine sugar
1 teaspoon ground cinnamon
grated zest and juice of
   1 unwaxed lemon
4 tablespoons orange flower
   water
115 g/4 oz. candied orange
   or mixed peel
1 large/US extra-large egg,
   separated
550 ml/generous 2 cups milk
175 g/6 oz. vermicelli
large pinch of sea salt
icing/powdered sugar,
   for dusting

28-cm/11-in. loose-bottomed
   flan tin

Serves 10

To make the pastry, sift the flour and sugar into a bowl and rub in the butter until the mixture resembles breadcrumbs. Make a well in the centre and add the egg, then gradually add the flour, mixing well to make a soft dough. Wrap in baking paper and chill in the fridge for 30 minutes.

To make the filling, put the ricotta, sugar (reserving 2 tablespoons), cinnamon, half the lemon zest, the lemon juice, the orange flower water, candied peel and the egg yolk in a bowl and beat together.

In a small saucepan, bring the milk to the boil. Add the vermicelli, salt, reserved sugar and remaining lemon zest and simmer gently until the vermicelli has absorbed nearly all the milk.

While it is still warm, stir the pasta carefully into the ricotta mixture. Whisk the egg white until it just holds it shape, then fold this into the mixture.

Preheat the oven to 170°C fan/190°C/375°F/gas 5.

On a lightly floured surface, roll out the pastry and use two-thirds of it to line the flan tin. It is a very short pastry, so it may tear but you can patch it very easily.

Spoon in the ricotta filling, then cut the remaining pastry into 5 mm/¼ in. strips and arrange them in a lattice pattern over the top of the tart.

Bake in the preheated oven for 40–50 minutes until golden. Dust with icing sugar before serving warm or cold.

DRUNKEN ALMOND & STRAWBERRY TART
UBRIACA DE FRAGOLE TORTA

Paestum, on the eastern edge of the Amalfi Coast (you can take a Sita bus there, south of Salerno), is famous for its Greek temples, buffalo mozzarella and strawberries. This is where this fine recipe originates from. Strawberries in this region are magnificent. This recipe is not quite a tart nor a cake but the best of both worlds. So utterly moreish and always, always so well received.

500 g/1 lb. 2 oz. strawberries, hulled
  and halved
2 tablespoons strawberry liqueur or
  Grand Marnier
6 large/US extra-large egg yolks (make
  sure to use the whites for other
  recipes), plus 1 for glazing
1 teaspoon vanilla extract
1 teaspoon almond extract
50 g/⅓ cup Italian '00' flour
1½ teaspoons baking powder
250 g/9 oz. ground almonds
  (ideally freshly ground)
200 g/1 cup caster/superfine sugar
grated zest of 2 unwaxed lemons
200 g/generous ¾ cup unsalted butter,
  plus extra for greasing

25-cm/10-in. loose-bottomed tart tin

Serves 8–10

Place the strawberries in a bowl and pour over the the liqueur. Chill and macerate for a least 1 hour.

Preheat the oven to 180°C fan/200°C/400°F/gas 6. Grease and line the base of the tart tin with baking paper.

Mix 6 of the egg yolks and the extracts together in a small bowl. Put the flour, baking powder, ground almonds, sugar and lemon zest in a food processor and mix to combine. Pour in the eggs and add the butter and mix together again. The mixture should be thick and creamy, but please don't over process.

Pour the batter into the prepared tart tin, level the surface with a palette knife and chill in the fridge for 20 minutes. Beat the remaining egg yolk and brush over the surface. Use a fork to make long squiggles on top.

Bake in the preheated oven for 12 minutes, then reduce the temperature to 160°C fan/180°C/350°F/gas 4 and bake for a further 20-30 minutes until golden. Leave to cool in the tin for 15 minutes, then remove and cool completely.

TONI'S ICE CREAM
BISCUIT TORTONI

Biscuit Tortoni is a creation of a Neapolitan ice cream maker, Mr Tortoni. Mr Tortoni expanded his career to Paris, where he opened the famous Café Napolitaine. This talented creator is popular throughout Italy.

300 ml/1¼ cups double/heavy cream
30 g/3½ tablespoons icing/powdered sugar
125 g/4½ oz. toasted chopped almonds
30 ml/2 tablespoons dark rum
225 g/8 oz. amaretti biscuits
10 maraschino cherries or cherries
  preserved in rum, or 10 fresh cherries

Serves 10

Arrange 10 paper cake cases on a baking tray or in a cupcake tray.

Whisk the cream and icing sugar together in a large bowl until stiff, then fold in the almonds and rum.

Break the amaretti biscuits into quarters and divide among the paper cases. Spoon the cream mixture over the biscuits and top with a cherry.

Place in the freezer for 1-2 hours until firm. Store in the freezer for up to 2 weeks.

COFFEE ICE CREAM

SPUMONE AL CAFFE

This is a Neapolitan ice cream made with cream, custard and ground coffee. Please use a good-quality ground coffee to get the best results – I like Kimbo and I grind it myself for a super fresh flavour. You will be surprised by the flavour combination, and I promise it is so delicious.

4 large/US extra-large egg yolks

100 g/½ cup caster/superfine sugar

¾ teaspoon ground cinnamon (the sweet version if you can find it)

3 tablespoons coarsely ground continental coffee

750 ml/3¼ cups double/heavy cream

Serves 6

Put the egg yolks, sugar, cinnamon and coffee in a heatproof bowl and beat well together.

Place the bowl over a saucepan of simmering water and using an electric whisk – or if very slowly, a balloon whisk – and whisk the mixture until it has doubled in volume. Remove the bowl from the heat and continue whisking until cool.

Whip the cream in another bowl until it holds its shape, then fold in the egg mixture.

Pour the mixture into an ice cream machine and freeze according to the manufacturer's instructions. This gives the spumone the best melt-in-your-mouth texture.

Alternatively, pour the mixture into a shallow freezer container and freeze, uncovered, for 1 hour until mushy. Turn the mixture into a chilled bowl and whisk until smooth. Return to the container, freeze again until mushy, then whisk again. Return to the freezer to become firm. Cover the container to prevent the spumone absorbing any other flavours.

MELON SORBET

SORBETTO DI MELONE

The sugar in this recipe can vary according to the sweetness of the melon. During the long hot summers in Italy, when people are prostrate with heat, lying about fanning themselves, a spoonful of melon can bring one back to life.

**2 ripe cantaloupe melons,
flesh cut into 2.5 cm/1 in. chunks
75-100 g/¹/₃-¹/₂ cup caster/superfine
sugar**

Serves 6

Pulse the melon in a food processor or blender until smooth. Add sugar to taste, which is a personal matter, starting with 75 g/¹/₃ cup.

Chill the purée for 2 hours, then churn in an ice cream machine. Alternatively, turn into a plastic tub, cover and freeze for 30 minutes, forking the mixture halfway through to prevent it freezing into a solid block. Store the sorbet in the freezer until ready to serve, then scoop into dishes and enjoy.

LIMONCELLO ICE CREAM

LIMONCELLO GELATO

Decadent and divine, this indulgent treat is so on-trend and is served all over Italy.

**finely grated zest and juice
of 3 unwaxed lemons
200 g/7 oz. icing/powdered sugar
450 ml/scant 2 cups double/heavy cream
3 tablespoons Limoncello, ice cold
from the freezer**

Serves 4

Put the lemon zest and juice in a large bowl, stir in the sugar and leave for 30 minutes.

Whip the cream with the Limoncello into soft peaks, then beat in the lemon juice mixture. Pour into an ice cream machine and churn. Alternatively, turn into a plastic tub, cover and freeze for 30 minutes, forking the mixture halfway through to prevent it freezing into a solid block.

LAYERED ICE CREAM DESSERT

CASSATA SEMIFREDDO

A famous Neapolitan gelato that will wow and impress guests, but most importantly it is delicious. Because of the intense heat in the summer, gelato becomes a vital food to cool and refresh the spirits. As a child, I loved the colourful array of gelato and found it very difficult to choose, so to have these three flavours in one is so intensely satisfying.

175 g/scant 1 cup golden caster/superfine sugar

2 large/US extra-large egg whites

600 ml/2½ cups double/heavy cream

1 vanilla pod/bean, seeds scraped out

200 g/7 oz. super ripe bright red strawberries

100 g/3½ oz. super ripe raspberries

1 tablespoon icing/powdered sugar

75 g/2¾ oz. dark chocolate, 75% cocoa solids

neutral oil, for oiling

900-g/2-lb. loaf tin
(11 x 22 cm/4½ x 8½ in.)

Serves 8

Lightly oil, then line the loaf tin with cling film/plastic wrap, leaving plenty of cling film overhanging.

Put the caster sugar in a saucepan with 4 tablespoons water, then heat gently until it has completely dissolved. Turn up the heat and boil for 2 minutes.

As the sugar comes up to temperature, whisk the egg whites to stiff peaks in a separate bowl. When the hot syrup is ready, carefully pour it into the egg whites, a little at a time, with the beaters still running, whisking until it has all been mixed in. Continue beating for 2 minutes until it has cooled, then set aside. The mixture should be mousse-like.

In another bowl, softly whip the cream and vanilla seeds together. Fold the cream into the egg whites in 3 batches to make the ice cream base. Divide the mixture between 3 separate bowls, making one of the batches marginally smaller than the others.

Blend the berries and icing sugar in a food processor or blender, then pass it through a sieve. Fold the fruit base into the smaller batch of cream base and mix to a beautiful pink colour. Spoon it into the lined tin and level the surface. Cover with a rectangle of baking paper and freeze for 30 minutes.

Remove the paper and spoon over the plain vanilla layer, levelling the surface. Cover and freeze as before.

Meanwhile, melt the chocolate in a bowl set over a pan of simmering water, then leave to cool.

Fold the cooled chocolate into the remaining ice cream base. Layer it in the tin, again covering with paper, and freeze for at least 3-4 hours before serving. Leave the semifreddo out of the freezer for 10 minutes to soften before serving cut into slices.

LEMON LIQUEUR

LIMONCELLO

I stumbled across *cicirinella*, which is a lemon, orange and aniseed-based liqueur made to a very secret recipe from a distant relation of my grandmother, the Mansi family. However, I must include this recipe, as it's magnificent. This liqueur is made throughout the whole of southern Italy. As flavour is so important, always use unwaxed lemons. In Italy, we use pure alcohol, which is difficult to obtain in the UK; a high proof vodka is a good alternative, as it has a neutral flavour. This liqueur is good after a meal if you like the sweetness, and some Italians love it poured over their gelato. My aunt makes it still, to her own specific recipe, and never reveals her secret ingredient (we think it's mint leaves...).

6 unwaxed lemons
750 ml/3¼ cups vodka (or pure alcohol)
225 g/8 oz. caster/superfine sugar
450 ml/scant 2 cups bottled filtered water

Serves 6

Put the lemons in a bowl of cold water and leave to soak for 1 hour. Remove from the water and dry with paper towels.

Use a vegetable peeler to carefully peel the rind from the lemons, taking care not to remove the white pith. Put the lemon rind in a wide-mouthed jar, pour over the vodka and cover. Leave in a dark place for 20 days.

After 20 days, put the sugar and bottled water in a saucepan and bring to the boil, stirring to dissolve the sugar. Remove from the heat, cover and leave until cold.

When cold, add the sugar mixture to the lemon zest mixture. Strain the mixture, pour into sterilized bottles and seal. Leave in a cold, dark place for 7 days before serving.

Serve cold and, once opened, store in the fridge.

FERRIGNO FAMILY APERITIF

FERRIGNO APERITIVO

This is a wonderful ice-breaking cocktail, which my grandfather insisted on serving at all family gatherings. I had it on offer at the launch of my last book!

2 tablespoons Limoncello
Prosecco, to top up
ice cubes
1 lemon slice
sprig of fresh mint

Serves 1

Pour the Limoncello into a large wine glass and top up with Prosecco.

Add the ice, lemon slice and mint and serve at once.

INDEX

PICTURE CREDITS

ACKNOWLEDGEMENTS

I am always reassured by Ryland Peters & Small, that a beautiful book will be created, and that is yet again what has happened, with a whole team of talent behind the scenes. *Mille grazie*.

This book has enabled me to dig a little deeper into the archives and family history. It has felt personal and emotional at times but the joy of putting together a collection of recipes, and the memories that have surfaced, has been fascinating.

Thank yous are owed to so many:
To Julia Charles, my commissioning editor, for her constant encouragement, good humour and passion.

Abi Waters, for spotting many, many inaccuracies, and her total dedication.

Working with Susan Fleming, the talent behind hundreds and hundreds of beautiful books, sitting with her, reminiscing and her gently coaxing information out of me for the essays has been a real highlight. Her knowledge and strength know no bounds.

Nassima, thank you for your stunning photography - it's exactly what I wished for.
To the food stylist Eleanor Mulligan, brava.

To Toni, for your wonderful design work and making the book look so beautiful.